For Cynthia + Stan

lots from

Gilbert + George
X   X

With Gilbert & George in Moscow

BY THE SAME AUTHOR

For James Birch

Gilbert & George dwarfed by the heroic sculpture of the Soviet worker and peasant girl by Vera Mouchina. The emblem of the hammer and sickle had been chosen in an artistic competition in 1922. Gigantic, metallic, and hollow, the statue caused a sensation when it was reassembled for the Paris Exhibition in 1925.

Photo. Daniel Farson.

WITH
GILBERT & GEORGE
IN
MOSCOW

by
Daniel Farson

BLOOMSBURY

First published 1991

Copyright © 1991 by Daniel Farson

The moral right of the author has been asserted

Bloomsbury Publishing Ltd, 2 Soho Square, London W1V 5DE

A CIP catalogue record for this book is available from the British Library

ISBN 0 7475 0952 2

Co-ordinated by Tyrone Dawson

Produced by Uwe Kraus GmbH, Murr

Printed in Germany

CONTENTS

ГИЛБЕРТ И ДЖОРДЖ
КАРТИНЫ 1983-1988
МОСКОВСКАЯ ВЫСТАВКА
28 АПРЕЛЯ ДО 1 ИЮНЯ
1990

Организованную Союзом художников СССР,
Джеймсом Берчем, Сергеем Клоковым
и Галерей Энтони д'Оффэ

Центральном Доме художника,
по адресу: Крымский вал 10, Москва

The Invitation

INTRODUCTION

On the flight home, the pilot of British Airways used to make the announcement, 'We are now leaving Russia'. I am told that the passengers cheered. Now that we have new sympathy for the problems of the Russians, I hope this boorish practice has been abandoned. Yet I admit I was relieved to leave Moscow airport where three stern-faced Soviet women denied any knowledge of my flight to Istanbul as they added to their heavy mauve make-up, even though the Turkish officials took over a few minutes later from the very same desk.

I admit, also, that I relished the luxury on the Turkish plane, the constant supply of excellent food and drink from a smiling stewardess, and the ample space, unlike the stained seats in Aeroflot which seem to be intended for smaller versions of Napoleon. There were only six of us on board so it resembled a private jet, with room to move about and introduce ourselves.

The man across the aisle, a moustachioed Turk, had a puppy on the seat beside him, alert though quiet, in a splendid, hand-made cage resembling a miniature Baalbek made of wood.

'That is an interesting dog,' I said fatuously, for it was an ordinary mongrel.

'Yes. This is special dog.' He explained that his two daughters were heartbroken after their beloved dog had been run over in Istanbul. Knowing where it came from, he had gone to the same part of Russia to find another which resembled it.

'This is my third daughter,' he told me proudly.

I sat back in my seat, a glass of raki in my hand, enchanted by such romantic folly. I was content, though prepared for the worst. Going through the notes I had made in the Caucasus, I had come across the scrawled entry: 'This is *too* perfect. Unless I have some bad luck soon, this will end in disaster.'

The plane did not crash as I half expected. I have the final recollection of that Russian toy dog, tail erect as it sidled through the Customs in Istanbul beside that squat, devoted Turk, towards two girls whose faces were alight with expectation as they waved to their father beyond the barrier. Lucky dog!

My own luck ran out with a bump a few days later south of Marmaris where I become involved with a strong-willed woman ... But that, as they say, is another story.

CHAPTER ONE

AT HOME IN FOURNIER STREET

'Gilbert & George are at the door,' said the nice night porter in the Fielding Hotel. 'Thank God!' I muttered inwardly, for this meant that I was on my way to Moscow. It had been a close-run thing, with the Russian Embassy playing their sadistic waiting game of withholding the visas (I needed two for I was continuing to Tblisi in Georgia) until the last moment.

Though assured by the d'Offay Gallery that this was usual, I wondered if the delay had anything to do with my first abortive journey on the *Krupskaya* where I upset the British Communists on the Peace Cruise by toasting the anniversary of the Czech uprising in the bar. After some heated words with the Captain, I was asked to leave the ship in Copenhagen. Did Soviet admirals keep a blacklist of 'undesirables'? Perhaps my identity festered in some Russian file, even in the changed conditions of perestroika, suddenly to be activated by my application to go to Moscow for Gilbert & George's exhibition which opened a week later on Friday 27 April 1990.

These foolish and decidedly vain thoughts haunted me as the hours ticked by, and at six o'clock when the offices closed down for the weekend, I abandoned hope and decided to return to my home in Devon.

I felt it was crucial that I should travel on the same flight as Gilbert & George, not only for the benefit of the feature I was writing for the *Sunday Telegraph* but also for my peace of mind. It would smack of failure if I had to follow on another flight a few days later.

Of course I did not go back to Devon and I was rewarded when I returned to my hotel at midnight to be handed a packet complete with 'itinerary', prepared by the Barry Martin Travel Agency which specialises in Russia, my numerous air tickets and my two visas.

Now it was dawn, never my favourite time of day, a few hours later.

'Gilbert & George are at the door.'

'In person?'

'Very much so.'

I was expecting them to wait in a hired limousine while a chauffeur or factotum was sent to fetch me. At that stage I did not know them well, and they stood there smiling, helping to carry my luggage to the taxi at the end of Broad Walk.

Their courtesy is unlike any other courtesy I know. I realised this as the day continued, an impression reinforced throughout the following week. I have known artistic people to turn on the charm like a garden hose, only to switch it off the moment the mood had passed. And I have known a few with genuine charm, like Graham Sutherland. The courtesy of Gilbert & George is something different and all the more startling to someone like myself who scarcely knew them but remembered the photographs with the puerile titles *George the Cunt* and *Gilbert the Shit*. Taken in 1969, these reflected their schoolboyish sense of mischief and the wish to shock. Their courtesy is the antidote: I do not know if they have always possessed it, or if they had to cultivate it. Even now, I am uncertain if a nastier creature lurks behind the mask, capable of violence and horrid outcry – after all, George bears a marked resemblance to Dr Crippen, or is it the murderer Christie?

I suspect the answer is simpler, as it is so often when we look for hidden depths with such determination that we find them when they do not exist: Gilbert & George are naturally courteous men.

I had met them once, at their home in Spitalfields in the East End of London where I went to interview them for my book *Gallery*, inspired by the television art quiz of the same name which I originated for Channel 4, with the artist Maggi Hambling on one panel, the art historian Frank Whitford on the other, and George Melly as the host. I choose the pictures and included one by Gilbert & George which created the usual controversy – they loved the living sculpture, hated the recent photo-pieces.

The arguments against them on *Gallery* seemed highly emotional and I thought then, as I have often thought since, that their critics expect Gilbert & George to deliver something they have no interest in delivering.

Conversely, a young Egyptian student at Oxford, Sepe Sehati, had photographed them for *Isis* where our profiles appeared adjacently, and had told me enthusiastically of their exceptional kindness. I arrived with an open mind.

Gilbert & George in the Brannam room at their London home.   Photo. Daniel Farson.

As I was early, I stopped for a drink at opening time at the pub on the corner. It proved a beastly pub with a Canadian landlord. This did not surprise me for I knew it by repute as the former Jack the Ripper which served a 'Ripper-tipple' cocktail to mark the anniversary of the murders in 1988, and for once I felt a sympathy towards the feminists who were so outraged that the brewers changed the name to something innocuous like The Three Bells. This has made it no less odious, nor the landlord more charming, as I discovered when I asked the way to Gilbert & George's house, interested to know how they were regarded locally.

'Oh, you mean the gay couple,' he scowled. Even then, I had the suspicion that no such label could be applied so glibly.

In contrast to the horrid pub, Fournier Street proved graceful – one of the last elegant streets remaining in the East End. It was built by and for the Huguenots, the French Calvinist Protestants who fled from religious persecution in France after the tolerance of the Edict of Nantes was revoked in 1685. Like other immigrants to the East End, they brought their skills, and these were more sophisticated than usual, especially in the manufacture of lace. Presumably they brought their money too, for Fournier Street was so exclusive that a barrier – like a frontier-gate – guarded the entrance to protect the residents from the *hoi polloi*.

Gilbert & George rented a ground floor in 1968 and were able to buy the freehold in 1974, restoring the dark wood panelling, scrupulously polished since by their cleaner and friend Stainton Forrest, and the spacious weaver-windows. 'People used to say it looked so nice empty,' George told Ed Mountfield, the interviewer from *Isis*. 'When everyone agrees like that they are usually wrong.' Instead, they have filled it with magnificent if overwhelming pieces of Barnstaple Art Pottery; Elton-Ware; Watcombe-Ware; and Christopher Dresser Art Ware pottery. My first impression was of bric-a-brac on shelves and glazed vases of Ali Baba proportions. With fine carpets, English neo-gothic furniture, tapestries, a Danby-like picture in a massive gilt frame of rocks in a stormy sea, and an Elizabethan portrait of 'a young person' – 'We like it because the figure could be either male or female,' said Gilbert – the effect verges on the meticulousness of a museum.

This was reinforced by my first impression of Gilbert & George, after their assistant Tyrone Dawson had shown me upstairs, asking if I drank coffee as if this was a rare ritual. They awaited me in their tight, three-buttoned tweed suits, made by the tailor next door, carefully posed as if for some Victorian photograph and, unless my memory is faulty, I believe that one was seated with the other standing beside the chair.

To start with, the conversation was equally 'Madame Tussaud's' as they assessed me, George with staring eyes behind his spectacles, Gilbert as nonplussed as Stan Laurel. I felt I was on trial – 'And when did you last see your father?' – and this was probably the case, for they are accustomed to the resentment of critics.

'The critics are 100 per cent against us,' said George, with a hint of satisfaction.

Though comparatively ignorant at this stage, I knew that few modern artists have been so reviled yet are so popular. Apart from winning the Turner prize at the Tate in 1986 they were given such prominence in the Royal Academy's exhibition of British Art in the Twentieth Century in 1987, with the gigantic photo-pieces *Wanker*, *Bummed* and *Prick Ass*, that Peter Fuller, editor of *Modern Painters*, condemned the organiser, Norman Rosenthal, for including their work, describing the artists as 'inconsequential'.

Though I grew to understand their work during our time in Moscow, I still find a disingenuousness – possibly calculated – in their indignation. With their choice of subject matter, usually phallic or narcissistic, applying to the young men in their photo-pieces as well as to themselves, they ask for trouble and I doubt if they are displeased when they get it.

As for the label 'fascist', like most labels this is too convenient. Neither am I sure what it means in their particular case. George explains it simply as 'a cliché applied to every person who doesn't fit'. As for the other label 'homoerotic', they stress that their work is deliberately restricted to male forms. 'If there were a poster for an exhibition called Nudes, people would assume they were female nudes,' said Gilbert. 'The male nude is still shocking,' George continued – for they speak in conversational relays – 'Nudes have always been women because men have the money; look at advertising. If a woman artist painted women, her work would not be described as lesbian.' They laughed as one at the hypocrisy.

'If women had the cheque books, art would be filled with naked men!' said George.

Because of the abundance of young men in their work, this is a theme that interviewers constantly return to. George told Gray Watson (*Artscribe*, 1987), 'Traditionally, it has been women illustrated and men wanking, looking. The popular understanding of the nude in art is a naked lady on a bed. The suppression of men which has resulted from the use of women as a symbol in this way is hideous beyond belief. If you open any one of hundreds of magazines on sale and see pictures of women, the message – for men – is always the same: that one day, if they're lucky, they'll get one of those beautiful girls.'

In a spirited interview for *Melody Maker* that same year they told Jim Shelley that they had given their lives away to art – 'We're the dead rabbit on the plate' – insisting that there was nothing homosexual in their work: 'All men have cocks. [*Cock* is a 48-inch by 59-inch erect penis.] We *are* interested in sex. We don't do eunuch art. There are no great eunuch artists. We don't want to decide what a person does with their hands or sexual organs. More importantly, we're normal.'

AT HOME IN FOURNIER STREET

When Ed Mountfield, of *Isis*, suggested that Clause 28 could lead to the banning of some of their more overtly homosexual pictures, he found that George became animated at last: 'We think the new legislation is unfortunate, but it was provoked. We were asked to sign a petition against it, and on it were the names of many of the very same critics who had gay-bashed us.'

George told me how he deplored the booklet, which showed 'Daddy in bed with another man' and stressed the stupidity of going into the street with a photograph of two men fucking, asking strangers, 'You do agree with this, don't you?'

Gilbert joined in, stressing that they like to be *subversive* but not to confront. 'All the people who have brought about Clause 28 have just made sexuality divisive, which is a very bad thing. After all, you don't need to know the sex of a piece of meat you are eating for dinner, do you? It is just meat. Or flowers; if you send a beautiful bunch of flowers, you don't check which one is spunking off with the next one.'

Sometimes, Gilbert & George indulge in disingenuousness, and enjoy expounding their philosophy even when it tempts them into making exaggerated pronouncements to the point of silliness, but in their detestation of gay militancy they are clear. Ironically, this loses them the support of the critics who might otherwise be in sympathy, as well as those who hate everything they stand for.

People who meet them for the first time are surprised to find that they do not fit the accepted role of today's 'gay', and are left confused. A well-meaning friend of mine in Devon exclaimed, 'They sound wonderfully camp!' when I described them, and I had to tell him that he could not have got it more wrong. They are true to themselves alone.

Though they claim to *deshock* as in defuse, there is no denying that they enjoy being provocative. And why not? How boring it would be if they were bland.

The moment they trusted me, they relaxed. George's staring eye turned naughty, Gilbert's started to glint. At this stage I thought of them in unison, as telepathic as twins, with the mutual understanding of a couple who have been inseparable for 24 years.

Later, in Moscow, I was delighted to recognise the differences which enhance their relationship. One midnight, at one of the many bedroom parties in the Ukraine Hotel, I asked George what he would do if anything happened to Gilbert.

'I'd be utterly lost,' he replied, and I have never seen him look so serious.

Gilbert & George on the rooftop of their house in Fournier Street with the spire of Hawksmoor's Spitalfields church behind them, and the chimneys inscribed with the name of William IV.

Photo. Daniel Farson.

Conversely, if anything happened to George, I suspect that Gilbert would close his life in England and return to northern Italy. I have no particular reason for thinking this, but I doubt if either would wish to continue working on his own.

When we first met they had the disconcerting habit of speaking in aphorisms. Then I realised that they are wildly funny, completely at variance with the unsmiling misery which they present as part of their carefully constructed façade. 'We think everyone is chasing pleasure, but you are more alive if you're miserable,' George assured me, and looked reproving when I laughed.

'Can there be humour in art?' I asked, warming to a favourite obsession. 'No more than there is in life.' And when I referred to Renoir's sensuous celebration of life in the scenes of friends and families lunching beside the Seine, George made the shrewd observation, 'Perhaps he *avoided* life.'

I referred to their picture *Coming,* with Y-fronts raining from the sky, suggesting that this might be considered humorous. 'Certainly not,' said George. 'And do you know, a critic said that all the underpants were *soiled.* Extraordinary!' He looked startled when I laughed.

Gilbert followed up with another show of indignation: 'Our pictures are no more provocative than life itself. We want people to behave differently after they've seen them. That's what we live for.'

'We know we're turning over stones,' George continued, 'but we don't seek to shock.'

I thought they protested too much, and Gilbert read my mind, pointing out that blatantly homoerotic pornography can be found in any dirty bookshop. 'We want to show the new possibilities of life, but people are intolerant towards the form we use. We accept this. We believe in truth. We hate so much the baggage of art – Greek columns, do you need it?'

Paradoxically, in their search for truth they alienate themselves from art, declining to go to galleries. 'We don't *like* art,' said Gilbert. 'we *do* it, they *look.*'

George agreed. 'Art has to come from life, not from art, and we appeal to young people who don't necessarily go to galleries. When students come to us we say their works is brilliant. "But you haven't seen it!" they exlaim. "It's not necessary," we tell them. "Support is the most important thing. Teachers always criticise."'

At this point, I was uncertain about their work. One thing disturbed me – was it painting? Working on photographic images with vivid dyes of reds, blues, yellows and greens, their technique is undeniably clever: a brilliant use of colour and combination of photographic blow-up and paint so the two are indistinguishable, with a finish that could hardly be improved. Yet then I wondered if this was cleverness to the point of sterility. At the same time, I saw the injustice of critics (what *is* the collective term for critics – a *grudge* of critics, perhaps?) who applaud such technique when practised by Warhol yet condemn it in Gilbert & George because of subject matter they find too disturbing to accept.

'English art critics have been Marxist,' they explain, 'and so narrow-minded. Art is there to bring out the prejudice. Our works brings out the bigot.' Devoting all the proceeds of their 1989 exhibition at the d'Offay Gallery to the treatment of AIDS, they commented that the *Guardian* is 'anti-gay only in our case; while the *Sun* has never gay-bashed us'.

We went on to the roof among the identical chimneys inscribed with the name of William IV, where I photographed them with the spire of Spitalfields Church in the background, and they continued with their catalogue of personal woe: wearing the same clothes every day ('to save our energy for art') and eating lunch and dinner at the Market Café on the corner of Fournier Street as they have done for the last twenty years, which serves the best English food according to George. 'We don't like fussy restaurants where every meal's a celebration. We like food as it used to be.'

Cringing from the thought of greasy chips (though I have gathered since that the caff serves excellent beef and roast potatoes) I asked what was a wrong with celebration?

'That would be selifish,' said George reprovingly. 'We wish to be left free for our art.'

'Theatre?'

'We don't like soothing art forms.'

'Friends?'

'None. We are completely free.'

I asked if they entertained and received a blast worthy of Lady Bracknell – 'Entertain? NEVER!'

Now that the photographs had been taken and the interview was over, we walked to the main road while they pointed out the new architecture which they liked. We took a taxi to the Groucho Club where we enjoyed the best of celebrations with lots of 'fussy food', and the company of James Birch.

CHAPTER TWO

JAMES BIRCH – THE CATALYST

Without the infinite patience of James Birch, the historic exhibitions of Francis Bacon and Gilbert & George would not have taken place in Moscow.

His looks are gentle, with amused blue eyes and a lock of fair hair falling over his forehead like an English school prefect. He dresses in loose black suits that are the height of tousled fashion, with soft white shirts and the occasional tie when protocol demands as it did in Moscow where appearances are all important. His handwriting is the illiterate scrawl of the upper classes.

The flopsy looks are deceptive because a fox lurks behind that puzzled smile, his 'niceness' redeemed by a ruthless impatience with those who cross or bore him.

The Russians saw him as a modern Lord Byron. When the mistress of a Russian artist called Anton offered him her teenage daughter James was shocked: 'Naively, she thought that if I'd gone to bed with the girl I'd have married her and got her out of Russia.' He had gone to dinner in the inevitable apartment block and the girl was offered as an inducement to stay behind – 'James, please stay, dance a little and then take your pleasure!' He refused but when he returned to the hotel the artist implored him to go back with him to the tenement on the outskirts of Moscow – 'For my sake, James, please.' As James is a kind man he agreed, but found the girl asleep clutching her teddy bear. She was woken up and produced in jeans and 'dreadful make-up' on the verge of tears. 'Don't worry,' James assured the girl, and caught a taxi all the way back to the hotel. 'I finally got to bed at seven in the morning, *utterly exhausted*!' In fact he has a daughter of his own, much the same age as the Russian girl.

His involvement with the art world was a natural development. He

James Birch in between Gilbert & George in Soho's Dean Street. The Birch & Conran Gallery behind them, marked by the clock, had to close in 1990 due to a massive rent increase. Photo. Daniel Farson.

studied the history of art at school, continuing at Aix-en-Provence University, before joining Christie's, where he served his apprenticeship at the front counter for six months before he moved to the Old Masters' picture department.

JAMES BIRCH – THE CATALYST

Today, his father, Simon Birch, works as a part-time consultant for Christie's in the City. His godfather is Sir John Pope-Hennessy, the former director of the British Museum and the Victoria & Albert, who now lives in Italy and who wrote an appreciative letter to his godson saying how wonderful he thought Gilbert & George were after seeing their work in Buffalo, a contrast to the usual disapproval of the art establishment.

Frustrated by not being allowed to start a rock-and-roll department in Christie's, James left after eighteen months to research the Fifties in America, 'which led to my interest in contemporary arts when I stayed three months in New York'. Back in London, he dealt in pictures from home, driving them to his clients until he was stopped by the loss of his licence for eighteen months after a drunken night out with Gilbert & George in 1982 on one of their first encounters. Looking for something to occupy his time, he opened an art gallery in the King's Road, where the launching parties were more memorable than the work of the young artists, which sold largely due to James's personal enthusiasm. A neo-naturist exhibition made news when Jennifer Binnie rode naked on a white horse through Chelsea on her way to the private view. The first exhibition showed the work of John Banting, and was visited by Gilbert & George in order to be supportive after their disastrous night out. It is interesting the way things go in circles, as James explained that Banting was a close friend of Brian Howard who introduced Francis Bacon to Muriel Belcher at the opening of the Colony Room in 1948, only two doors away from the Birch & Conran Gallery which James started with Paul Conran in 1987.

I met James for the first time in the Colony when it was run by Ian Board after Muriel's death, and warmed to his enthusiasm and constant capacity to surprise. Our friendship was consolidated when he gave me a photographic exhibition in the summer of 1988; it included the portraits I had taken for *Picture Post* of Salvador Dali, Brendan Behan, Noel Coward and Robert Graves, and 'rediscovered' me as a photographer. This gave me first-hand experience of his quiet skill yet innate modesty that is at variance with the more bombastic ventures in the King's Road.

James has told me, 'The Russian connection began in 1985 at a party where I met Robert Chenciner, who asked me what I was doing. When I said I hoped to take ten young artists to New York, he asked "Why not take them to Moscow instead?" As I had no idea what to do, he advised me to go to the Soviet section of UNESCO in Paris and meet a man called Sergei Klokhov. When I met him I was riddled with flu and found myself in the middle of the Soviet delegation which was celebrating, as the Russians always seem to do, and no one was sure why I was there. I had lunch with Sergei Klokhov and Elena Khadiakova, who changed her clothes between courses – a disco outfit for the avocado pear; evening dress with the steak and frites. Because I was so dazed by flu I couldn't understand what was going on until I discovered that Elena was a fashion designer who was trying to impress me – though God knows why!

'It was over lunch that Klokhov told me to send a protocol letter to Moscow about the young artists, which I did. I heard nothing for nine months. Then I received a telegram: "We like your proposals. Come VIP. Arrive as soon as possible." Luckily I could afford the fare as I was closing the King's Road gallery, and arrived with Robert Chenciner.

'In those days we had to go in a delegation and were lumped with two people from the *National Geographic* though our projects were entirely different, and we stayed together at the National. All the buildings were covered with Soviet slogans and red hammer and sickle flags, which added some colour to Moscow compared to the drabness today. Sadly all that stuff has gone now – I found it rather exciting.'

On the way to the National, Klokhov warned James that the Union of Artists were fed up with the British because nothing ever happened with cultural exchange. Fortunately, the official involved had broken a ski and Klokhov had been able to repair it in Paris, so the man owed him a favour: 'Now I will see Mr Birch.'

Within two days after meeting members of the Union of Artists, James realised that the idea of bringing ten young artists to Russia was out of the question as they were not ready for them. He noticed when he visited the artists' studios that they were desperately keen in Moscow to see the work of Francis Bacon, and that this would blaze the trail for further Western exhibitions.

Used to dealing with stuffy, middle-aged bureaucrats, the Russians were surprised to find that James was so young, for he was still in his twenties, and he returned with nothing arranged but invaluable goodwill.

Entirely by chance, I happened to be present at the conception of the Francis Bacon exhibition when a group of us, including Francis, moved on one evening from the Colony Room to the Trattoria Terrazza further down Dean Street. When this was run by Franco and Mario it was a place to look forward to; by now it had been taken over by Kennedy Brooke who had spoiled Francis's favourite restaurant, Wheeler's, around the corner in Old Compton Street, and the atmosphere in Dean Street began to curdle as we endured an indifferent meal situated in a corner surrounded by piping. The conversation was less than sparkling in consequence, until James remembered the Russian interest in Bacon's work which had been overlooked during the excitement of opening his new gallery.

James asked Francis if he would consider exhibiting his work in Moscow and was startled by the enthusiastic reaction. Giving James his private telephone number, he asked him to call the next morning and confirmed his support. James said later, 'I rang Klokhov in Moscow and said would you be interested? He rang me back and said yes. From that date it took me two years to arrange, going backwards and forwards to Moscow four or five times.'

If James was the initiator on this side, Klokhov was the fixer in Russia. Looming on the horizon, he was a catalyst too, though more formidable than James; an official power behind the scenes and a brilliant manipulator, guiding him through the maze of red tape which doesn't come redder than it does in Moscow.

The antidote to James's modesty, the bearded Sergei would make a splendid Svengali in a stage production of *Trilby*. Owner of a snake farm in Uzbekistan, which sports scorpions as well as 30 cobras that supply venom, he is not a man to disregard. He knew the protocol precisely: 'There are so many bureaucratic parties involved and a letter can stay on one person's desk for up to two months unless you know exactly how to get things moving. Seeing the person you are dealing with is enormously important in Russia.'

James heeded his advice and gradually won the trust of the Russians, who recognised his integrity. He had greater difficulty in England, not with the Marlborough Gallery which handles Bacon's work, but with the British Council who saw the prestige involved and started to take the show over. Though he was the instigator, they gave James less than his due, even omitting his name from the official documents, which Sergei had to fight to replace, a slight from the Council that James has not forgiven. After the exhibition, the British Council sent James a cheque for £8 for having brought out their Visitor's Book which they had forgotten: 'Later they expressed sadness at my article in *Modern Painters* in which I reinstated my role. I wrote back after their letter was published admitting it was not all down to me, yet in one sense it was for they completely forgot how it was set up and the cost to me personally of setting it up. They realised their mistake and sent me a cheque for my air fare to the opening.'

Knowing none of this, I found the British Council helpful in offering to pay for my own flight to Moscow to help me cover the Bacon exhibition for the *Daily Mail*, who would pay for the rest of my expenses. Naturally I was excited, and so was everybody else at this penultimate stage, Bacon as much as anyone, until the mood changed.

One evening in the Groucho Club, also in Dean Street, I met Francis Bacon in the back of the bar and seldom have I seen him look so testy. I was shocked when he told me that he doubted if he would go to Moscow after all. The reason was not entirely clear; basically he suspected that he was being taken advantage of. He had lunched with a couple from the British Council, a husband and wife, and found their complacency so boring he had refused to allow them to pay the bill as they wished to do, paying it himself as a form of inverted punishment.

I could understand this. I had struggled with a feature on the British Council commissioned by *The Times*, having various meetings with officials who were friendly yet so tedious that I felt I was drowning slowly in a sea of platitudes, and abandoned the whole idea.

Now James was being criticised for failing to explain the problems of the protocol involved and it seemed that Francis had turned against his participation in principle, and, though I doubted if he used the actual word, his various complaints amounted to the suspicion that he was being 'conned'.

For once I was restrained and sensed that it could prove ruinous if I urged him to go ahead regardless. I did my best to reassure him that James had behaved impeccably throughout, and sympathised over the boredom of the couple from the British Council, stressing, 'You must do exactly as *you* want. That is all that matters. If you don't want to go, don't.'

'Well, I don't.'

'Of course the young Russian artists will be disappointed.'

'That's rubbish!' he told me emphatically. 'They know my work already. They send me letters. They don't need to see me.'

I laughed nervously. 'You know, you might enjoy it.'

'I doubt that greatly.'

'They'd be so glad to see you that you could do what you wanted; they could even hold the press conference without you...'

'Press conference!' he cried, as if I had upset my drink over him. Oh God, I thought, he doesn't realise that this will be part of the jamboree, even though it was listed in the British Council's itinerary. I could see my own chances of reaching Moscow receding.

'What press conference?' he repeated, his voice echoing his vexation.

I explained that, conceivably, just possibly, the artist might be expected to say a few words, adding that this would be quite unnecessary in his case. 'You must do exactly as you like.'

Gilbert & George with the maquette which they prepared after their first visit to Moscow when they took the measurements of the rooms in the New Tretyakov Gallery. Supervising every stage of the exhibition personally, they left nothing to chance.   Photo. Daniel Farson.

'Anyhow,' he concluded, 'there's my asthma.' He explained that this had been worse recently, yet told me in slight contradiction that he was delighted that his doctor hoped to travel to the exhibition too, so there was nothing to worry about should there be a further attack in Moscow.

'But Francis, if you're suffering from asthma, the flight could be disastrous.' Having raised the issue, he dismissed it: 'I don't know, it's just a few hours. We'll see.'

Perhaps his mind was resolved already, for I have never known him change it after he reaches a decision. In due course, asthma became the official alibi accompanied by a message of personal regret, and I returned the cheque for my flight to the British Council for my story was no longer valid without the presence of Francis Bacon.

From what I have learnt since, I underestimated his original enthusiasm which had prompted him to learn Russian from a cassette for the six previous months. James has told me how he set out for Moscow with John Edwards, Bacon's close friend who was representing him and whose portrait adorned both the poster and the catalogue. 'We had bacon and eggs in his studio and you could tell that Francis was excited and John said, "I bet if he'd had a visa he would have hopped on the plane with us".'

Someone faltered somewhere along the line. The British contingent to Moscow included Lord Gowrie, our former Arts Minister, and Henry Meyric-Hughes, the director of the British Council's Fine Arts Department, who attended the obligatory press conference. But the artist himself was absent.

This made Gilbert & George's impending arrival all the more welcome.

Apart from liking them personally, James was convinced that Gilbert & George were the natural follow-up to the Bacon exhibition. 'It was my theory that the Russians were used to social realism and would find Gilbert & George similar, and that this would make the exhibition popular: neither difficult, nor abstract, but art for all and easy to understand. I could not have been more wrong! They were sick of social realism, having had it rammed down their throats for years. Fortunately they loved Gilbert & George anyhow.'

James had once compared their work to me as the equivalent of Russian icons – large, powerful, figurative – and I came back to this saying that it was a nice phrase but what did it mean?

'It's not just a phrase. Gilbert & George's work has that stained-glass icon feel, that religious feeling which the Russians could appreciate.'

One could also make a comparison to Renaissance ceilings, though when I mentioned the stained glass to Gilbert he was unimpressed: 'I think it is closer to computer games – space invaders.'

James's instinct led him to propose the Gilbert & George exhibition to Thair Salakov, the President of the USSR's Union of Artists, only two days after the opening of the Bacon, which attracted a thousand visitors a day. 'I knew, also, how greatly they wanted to exhibit in Moscow.'

Again it proved a gradual process, but this is where James excels. One night in the Ukraine Hotel during one of the midnight feasts in James's bedroom, Anatoly Ryzhnikhov (known to us as 'Herbert Lom's brother' because of his physical resemblance) explained James's approach: 'He does not push, push, he is very gentle man; a beautiful person. I receive hundreds of letters but I deal with James because of the trust. Finally, I said let us see the work, and I was impressed.'

Meanwhile, the beautiful Elena Khadiakova, who was staying with James in London, was instrumental in helping to persuade Sergei Klokhov that Gilbert & George would be right for the next exhibition.

On 16 July 1989, James flew to Moscow with Gilbert & George so that they could take the measurements of the gallery for their maquettes and meet the officials involved. The three of them formed a close relationship, bonded by their schoolboyish sense of humour. After collapsing in his hotel bedroom at dawn, James would be woken by a cheerful call from George asking him to hurry up and join them in the breakfast room, where George confronted him with a revolting Russian sausage. 'Delicious donkey dick!' he'd enthuse to the wilting James. 'After we've finished, we'll go upstairs and do our jobbies and meet downstairs in fifteen minutes.' Luckily, they shared a sense of absurdity, evolving a secret language which continued to convulse them in Moscow, though it mystified me. A sudden cry of 'oy!' would set them off, translated as a palindrome of black New York's 'yo!', an aggressive form of 'hey you, brother' and corruption of the skinhead chant 'oy-oy'. Unable to unravel this myself, I looked on with a strained and baffled smile as cries of 'oy!' united them.

The 1989 visit strengthened James's particular friendship with Mikhail Mikheyev – known as Misha Number One for there were several Mikhails – the Head of Art Promotion in the Union of Artists who did much in spreading the word that Gilbert & George were acceptable. Indeed, looking back, it seems astonishing that they were accepted so easily.

'Presumably some of the titles will have to be changed?' I asked them. With a sly smile George feigned surprise, so I suggested that

Queer, *Smash the Reds*, *Fucked Up* and *Bollocks We're all Angry* might need some explaining or might even cause offence.

George was perfectly aware of this and I learnt that the title of the poster *Shag* was translated as 'a small furry animal', and that *Coming*, with the Y-fronts falling from the sky, was retitled *Orgasm* and then finally to *Arriving*, which prompted a serious Russian student at the opening to interpret the raining underpants as an invasion from the West.

'Extraordinary!' said George, using a favourite word. It was during the 1989 visit that he asked Mrs Mikheyev if she preferred *Blooded* or *Shitted*. When she chose *Blooded*, George exclaimed, 'Aha! All women say that!'

On this first visit to Moscow, they were unaware that the British Council was unsympathetic towards the exhibition, even though it is their brief to promote the work of British artists abroad. With a minuscule annual budget for Russia estimated at a mere £20,000, such reluctance would have been understandable if they had been more diplomatic. With a staggering lack of tact, a top official in the British Council revealed the extent of their hostility by asking the Russian organisers why they were promoting the work of 'two homosexual fascists'?

If he hoped to frighten the Russians into cancelling the exhibition, this person underrated them. The Russians shrugged off this amazing statement as a devious example of bureaucracy with which they were all too familiar.

In fact the accusation was inflammatory. Though it has never been published, the rumour reached me in London that Gilbert & George intended to sue the British Council, and I asked them if this was true. Suddenly discreet, they told me they were unable to comment – 'It's all in the hands of the Council for Civil Liberties.' Should the case ever come to court, it promises to be the funniest litigation since Whistler sued Ruskin for accusing him of flinging a pot of paint in the public's face.

Undeterred by the British Council's attitude, Anthony d'Offay and Gilbert & George went ahead on their own at an estimated cost of £ 135,000.

Motivated by the hope of encouraging goodwill between the two countries, which can be achieved more lastingly by a great sporting or artistic event than by a hundred political speeches, James was shocked by such deviousness. 'I knew it existed in Russia; instead I found it coming from England.'

JAMES BIRCH – THE CATALYST

Where did I stand in all of this? Until my experience of the Moscow exhibition I was uncertain about Gilbert & George, not the artists but their work. When I wrote critically about their inclusion in the Royal Academy's exhibition of British Art in the Twentieth Century in 1987, this was a first reaction to something new. Later I was stunned by the impact of their work when I saw it at the d'Offay, and began to accept that they were reinventing the language of paint, largely by discarding the restrictions of brush and canvas and paint itself. Painting transcends language, or should do unless hidebound by the country it belongs to. Gilbert & George insist that their work is equally understandable in the African jungle – 'We want to provide the opportunity for people to feel new freedoms.' It is one of their strengths that each viewer sees a Gilbert & George picture differently.

However, as someone accustomed to the convention of brush and canvas I had gone to Fournier Street with my own preconceived prejudices as well as those of others.

CHAPTER THREE

WHO ARE GILBERT & GEORGE?
LEARNING MORE ABOUT THEM

WHAT IS YOUR IDEA OF PERFECT HAPPINESS? Being miserable
WHAT IS YOUR GREATEST FEAR? Being happy

Sunday Correspondent questionnaire

Gilbert & George are not what they seem. They surround themselves with such a smokescreen that it is hard to know who they are. I suspect this is what they wish.

Like the victim of a murder whose relatives, friends and lovers give conflicting descriptions to the police, they mean different things to different people.

Some people dislike them for reasons of their own: political, sexual, whatever... As for their constant assurance that they are miserable – 'We're the most miserable sods we know,' says one; 'the most miserable sods in the world,' agrees the other – I believe they persist in this like the pig-baby in *Alice* because they know 'it teases'. It can be a tiresome affectation, but even if they are having a joke at our expense – and sometimes I think they are – their 'miserable' façade is at least consistent. They may well be sincere when they believe that '*everyone* is desperate', and, conceivably, they could be right. 'We don't do anything for pleasure,' George told me once. 'I thought you were going to be nice today, Daniel, and here you are talking about pleasure.'

So who are they? I tried to get closer.

'We are nearly 100,' George told me, referring to themselves as one.

George was born in Plymouth in 1942, educated at Dartington Hall and the Oxford School of Art. His birthday is 8 January, which happens to be my own. Gilbert was born the following year in the Dolomites, north of Venice. He speaks of this mountainous part of Italy with affection, as if it were a separate republic, and has shown me nostalgic snaps of himself as a boy looking every bit as perky as he does today, surrounded by his brother and three doting sisters. 'From the age of fourteen I have always supported myself,' he says, though this did not prevent his pursuit of art, studying for three years at art school in Italy, one in Austria, and six in Munich, before he came to England to study at St Martin's – 'the most progressive art school in the world. I had to be where it was happening.'

It happened beyond expectation, for it was at St Martin's that he met George and became half of the most celebrated duo in the history of art.

'We were friends before we decided anything. George was the only person interested in speaking to me in pidgin English ...'

'Sign language,' George corrected him, and Gilbert grinned. 'My theory is that he *likes* foreigners!' as if this was the most astonishing trait in an Englishman, as indeed it is.

'It just came over us,' said George, referring to their partnership. 'People pointed out to us that we were working together.'

'We think it's normal,' said Gilbert.

At this moment I had an irresistible and affectionate image of Gilbert & George climbing up the ladder to Noah's Ark, in line with the other animals going in two by two.

George's childhood was less happy than Gilbert's. Though Dartington was a progressive school, I think that his subversive attitude made life there difficult.

'Father left home before I was born,' George told me, describing a bizarre episode at the age of 21 when he tried to track his father down. 'I remembered his name and address on the back of a postcard I found in our home – Rose Cottage, Dulverton. I always imagined a loving Daddy ... I knocked at the front door and it was answered by a lady ... I hadn't thought he might be married. She told me he was in the pub, where the barmaid pointed him out, "It's that man over there." And I said, "Excuse me, it's a bit personal, could we have a word in the other bar?" "Yes, but in here." I said, "Please, let us go to the other bar" at least ten times, at which point the bar was incredibly quiet and I gave up. "My name's George, I believe I'm your son." "Good lord! Let's go to the other bar!"'

And that is all that George is prepared to divulge about his family. I suspect the memory hurts – he had told me of this encounter before – and it helps to explain the bond with Gilbert and his concern for other people which is protective when it comes to the young. I gather that he did not see his father again.

WHO ARE GILBERT & GEORGE?

With George growing up fatherless, and Gilbert now deracinated (his own father died in 1988), they have that vital vulnerability. I have always noticed that the people I like the most have never grown up, like Lindsay Anderson and George Melly, and now count Gilbert & George among them. It means they are ageless, with all the zest of students.

The Living Sculpture they developed when they left St Martin's was born of necessity, for they were broke and unable to afford artists' materials. Covering their faces with red or gold paint was secondary to their extraordinary dedication, for they still performed when the room was empty, as George Melly describes later. Performance Art may be limited, but such single-mindedness gained them recognition a year after leaving St Martin's.

'It was not a conscious decision – something that happened – wanting to express ourselves with *nothing*!'

'The meaning of the song *Underneath the Arches* was very important,' said George. 'We were very close to being down-and-out ourselves. Literally we had no money. Suddenly we were no longer students, nor goody-goody ex-students who got tuition jobs; we had no contacts in the art world, yet we still wanted to be artists every day. A group show called When Attitudes Become Form had a travelling show and local artists were invited. We weren't, so we went along as Living Sculpture to the opening and became an extraordinary success. Konrad Fischer, probably the most famous art dealer in the world at that moment, happened to be there that night at the ICA. That one evening transformed our whole life – not doing art like other artists. We were the form and the content rolled into one.'

Gilbert took over: 'I think it was a revolution for us – and we're still doing it!'

George: 'Form – meaning – all entwined – that's what we still do. Only the form is different. People see the work like a letter to themselves. Each sees it differently. We must allow for every difficult, sad and sweet person.' (George is one of the few people I know who frequently uses the word 'sweet'.) I asked if being broke had been healthy for them.

'We believe so, that's why we always try to make ourselves broke.' I pointed out that the experience could have made them mean and bitter.

George: 'That's the reason.'

Gilbert: 'We like to push our ideas more openly and without our *own* money we couldn't do it. If we don't have any tomorrow, we'd have to do it another way. We believe art helps people, and money helps to bring art to the people.'

'We're very ruthless and practical,' adds George.

WHO ARE GILBERT & GEORGE?

From the outset they have relished declarations. In *The Laws of the Sculptors*, 1969, they stated four laws:

1. Always be smartly dressed, well groomed, relaxed, friendly, polite, and in complete control.
2. Make the world believe in you and pay heavily for this privilege.
3. Never worry, assess, discuss, or criticise but remain quiet respectful and calm.
4. The Lord chisels still, so don't leave your bench for too long.

In 1970, Gilbert & George, the sculptors, say:

WE ARE ONLY HUMAN SCULPTORS

We are only human sculptors in that we get up every day, walking sometimes, reading rarely, eating often, thinking always, smoking moderately, enjoying enjoyment, looking, relaxing to see, loving nightly, finding amusement, encouraging life, fighting boredom, being natural, daydreaming, travelling along, drawing occasionally, talking lightly, tea drinking, feeling tired, dancing sometimes, philosophising a lot, criticising never, whistling tunefully, dying very slowly, laughing nervously, greeting politely and waiting till the day breaks.

They followed this up the same year with the notorious double-portrait *George the Cunt and Gilbert the Shit*. They were on their way.

The first exhibition had taken place in Frank's Sandwich Bar in London in 1968. The following year they had released the first of their postal sculpture with 'Art for All' written at the top of the card, with the delightful inscription underneath: *All my life I give you nothing and still you ask for more* (the meaning of which has been analysed in excruciating depth by their admirers in Germany), signed by 'the sculptors George and Gilbert.' With roses in their lapels, and matching handkerchiefs, they look touchingly youthful and high-spirited, as they did the year before, sprawled, laughing on the rooftop of St Martin's, 'relaxing'.

Why had they chosen their first names George and Gilbert, later changed to Gilbert & George?

'We never thought that we should cling to our father's names for the rest of our lives,' said George. 'I only knew mine for twenty minutes.'

WHO ARE GILBERT & GEORGE?

'It's easier to remember,' said Gilbert, 'that's the point.' And a valid point too. Names are important: those of Francis Bacon, Lucian Freud, and Gilbert & George command instant attention. That of Kurt Schwitters, less so.

In 1971 their *Nature Photo Pieces* were shown at the Konrad Fischer Gallery in Düsseldorf; *The Evening Before the Morning After* followed at the Nigel Greenwood Gallery in London, with *Any Port in a Storm* at the Sonnabend Gallery in Paris in 1973.

Nigel Greenwood supported them in the early days, encouraging them to perform their Living Sculpture at his studio in Glebe Place, Chelsea, and subsequently exhibited their work seven times during the 1970s.

A startling panoramic photograph of their retrospective exhibition at the Düsseldorf in 1981 reveals how far they had advanced. Deserving close examination, it shows the diversity of their work, as if they had broken free from all restraints. This was repeated with similar retrospectives at the Pompidou in Paris, 1981; the Whitechapel, 1981; the São Paulo Biennale, 1981 (sponsored, surprisingly, by the British Council); the Sonnabend in New York, 1983; the Baltimore Museum of Art, 1984; and the Guggenheim Museum in New York, 1985. They have been exhibited throughout the world, with the exception, so far, of China and South Africa, though both are being considered at this moment.

Their first exhibitions with d'Offay took place in 1972; their first in his modern gallery in 1980.

With a liberal sprinkling of phallic symbols, the crucifix, and four-letter words in juxtaposition, they were determined to shock from the outset.

Gilbert insists, 'Art has to be subversive', and George agrees, 'Every picture we make is subversive. We can't shout this in the streets or we'd be arrested. This encourages the label of "fascist" but can also be seen as a retaliation against the Blackshirt Marxists who always want to dictate their morals to everyone. That's exactly what they are themselves. They love the word NO. No to this, no to that, no to the poll tax. They strangle the freedom of the artist. We're not allowed to misbehave any more. We are not allowed to be extreme.'

Then Gilbert added the devastating phrase 'The levellers are all about us'; devastating, because it is so true.

'The only interesting thing about this,' said George, referring to the 'fascist' label, 'is that if people are concerned about something and our pictures bring this out, then our art is doing its job. I believe we're exactly the opposite of fascist. So much modern art dictates, but everyone is free to see whatever they want in our work. Fascism is a cliché applied to every person who doesn't fit. It's what children call their parents when they can't get what they want.'

'You hear it in every sitcom,' Gilbert agreed. 'It's very silly.'

'Fascism came out of socialistic politics and we're boring conservatives,' George concluded. 'We don't mind being called fascist but not as an insult. There's nothing we haven't been called, in any case.'

Gilbert may complain that they are not allowed to misbehave but this does not deter them. He relishes the bad behaviour of others, especially George's, and is not averse to treading dangerously himself. Both have been arrested for being drunk and disorderly, though on separate occasions. Gilbert was the first and found it a 'terrifying' experience with the Black Maria and an appearance in court: 'I thought I was going to be raped!'

'That's Gilbert's definition,' George remarked self-righteously with a lift of the eyebrows. 'Obviously he went about it in the wrong way and must have upset the poor police. Very silly.'

'But *you*,' Gilbert intervened, spluttering with indignation. 'You were arrested yourself only a week later.'

'That's perfectly correct,' said George.

'How would you cope with prison?' I asked Gilbert.

'I *love* it!' he replied gleefully as he looked around the room in Fournier Street.

'Have you been mugged?'

'Both of us,' said George. 'We don't care about it – we call it "self-service dole".'

WHAT IS YOUR GREATEST REGRET? Not having discovered bad behaviour earlier in life.

They've had a go. Liam Carson, the courteous manager of the Groucho Club and a good friend to all of us, recalls an evening in the mid-Seventies when he worked in the Covent Garden bar Blitz which Gilbert & George visited, with George claiming that the house claret was superior to that of Simpsons. 'It was an odd place, not at all busy and the other "regulars" were young men from the East End who ran ice cream and other pitches along Oxford Street. One evening these young men held a birthday party. There were about 20 to 30 of them, including girlfriends. Gilbert & George were also dining. I don't know quite what sparked it off, I presume Gilbert & George made a pass or improper suggestion to one of the young men, but a barroom brawl that would have done justice to a Wild West saloon proceeded to take place. The

East End boys' homophobic rage knew no bounds and Gilbert & George – especially Gilbert – took a severe beating.

'We eventually managed to control it and I took them to the kitchen to clean up. Gilbert was badly cut – I think the result of a bottle over the head – but appeared more worried about spoiling his suit.

'The evening eventually subsided and Gilbert & George went off after paying their bill and leaving an extraordinarily large tip! I have spoken to them subsequently about the evening, and although they were the worse for wear they do recollect it. Since then, although the evenings have thankfully not been quite so explosive, they are never dull.'

Conversely, as Stainton Forrest has confirmed, there are no complaints on the morning after when they resume work.

Though they may appear 'woolly' (BBC Critics' Circle) to those who don't know them, and rather dotty even to those who do, they have never ceased to surprise me with their efficiency. They have the gifts of single-mindedness and simplicity. They know what they want and they are determined to get *that*, but they are happy to leave it there. They hate unnecessary excrescence, but this baffles those who are used to deviousness.

'What do they get out of it?' I am asked about various projects.

'Exactly what they say.'

'But they might be able to get more.'

'They don't want more.'

'Then there must be a snag?'

'No.'

They care passionately about their work.

WHEN AND WHERE WERE YOU HAPPIEST? Sober in our studio

HOW WOULD YOU LIKE TO BE REMEMBERED? As the artists we are

With no concept of the finished picture, they know exactly the human subject and area of thought and feeling which the picture will deal with. They discuss their methods openly with no attempt to inflate them with mystery. Putting the evolution of a picture as simply as I can: they start by taking a large number of photographs – as many as 30,000 – over a period of three months. These include views of London, especially Spitalfields where they live – Petticoat Lane, *after* the market had closed, provided one memorable shot taken from above – and portraits of themselves and sundry young men in their studio. The films are developed and contact sheets are printed which spark off ideas for possible subjects, with similar themes marked on different sheets. Then they enlarge the relevant negatives on to the largest and strongest photographic paper available, and subsequently dye the prints with one of the colours – hairy; flesh; pink; poor blue – stacked and labelled neatly in their spacious workroom behind the house in Fournier Street, each tub adorned by a pair of red rubber gloves. When they do the colouring they have assistance. Then the series of prints are mounted and framed into individual panels – up to 100 – and these are assembled into the finished collage of the picture.

Richard Dorment describes the process as arduous and complicated; Brian Sewell makes the observation that 'the amount of sheer drudgery is appalling and there can be no room left for art'.

Conversely, it shows that no one else could do the work as they conceive it.

Sewell claims, 'Gilbert & George have never been able to paint or draw or sculpt – but I do not blame them for taking the charlatan's way out when they so desperately wanted to be taken for artists after such long apprenticeships at public expense.' This ignores Gilbert's years at art school in Italy, Austria and Germany before he came to St Martin's, and their gifts as draughtsmen with their charcoal pieces which may well have influenced Kiefer – for good or for bad – when he saw them in Düsseldorf.

'We never take holidays,' they claim, 'we're not readers. We have a highly developed sense of purpose. When we are producing something we work round the clock and sometimes a bit more.'

Taking them literally, I suggested that if they cut themselves off from life, their art might be poorer.

'The more you see the less you're in a position to form life. We're interested in a new world: tomorrow's, not today's, and you can only do that in isolation. We really believe that. If you reflect reality, that's an illustrator's job.'

'How do you see the future?'

'One vision,' said Gilbert, 'the humanity of life.'

'We don't want to "think up" anything,' said George.

'It's more an evolution,' Gilbert continued. 'We're not artists who want to do something new every day, if at all!'

'We're deeply miserable,' said George, stuck in the grooves of that particular record. I asked if this belief of 'the desperate unhappiness of everyone on the planet today' was a barrier to hide behind?

'It's completely truthful.'

'But you're not miserable!' I protested.

'I shouldn't be too sure of that, said George, warningly.

'The façade is when we laugh,' laughed Gilbert. 'You've got to be miserable to produce such happy work. An artist becomes more and more dead, while the art becomes the living force. Artists look like dead people. People consider art in terms of a lifetime – every artist has a last picture. The pictures are alive but the artist becomes more and more dead. We look like dead fish.'

George: 'If we fell under a bus, the pictures would go on – they would be us.'

'At the beginning,' I asked, 'did you seek to sublimate, even lose your individualities, as Wolf Jahn has suggested?'

'We will agree with that. It's the giving that we want, not to get something. All the greatest writers and artists give. That's why they all had such unhappy lives.' They admit they were glad to accept the Turner prize from the Trustees of the Tate 'for services to British art' in 1986 because it irritated everyone, adding with a hint of satisfaction, 'we were the favourites of William Hill the bookmakers.'

'Would you accept knighthoods?'

'If it upsets people.'

In stripping their lives to the essentials, they have gained a freedom: they are not obligated to anyone. Equally, you do not have to pretend with Gilbert & George; you can be true to yourself, which is rare in any relationship. They may have only a few friends but this is their deliberate choice. I have found myself that as I grow older there are fewer people I regard as real friends, but I like those people all the more. In restricting their friendships, Gilbert & George enhance the lives of their circle. Going against the grain of today's cynicism, I doubt if they would betray either their country or their friends. 'We're rather moral as regards our heritage,' says George. Highly unfashionable.

WHAT IS YOUR GREATEST EXTRAVAGANCE? Treating younger people

WHAT IS THE TRAIT YOU MOST DEPLORE IN YOURSELF? Level-headedness

WHAT IS THE TRAIT YOU MOST DEPLORE IN OTHERS? Negativism

That they do not pursue happiness does not preclude it, but they have the sense to know it is not a substance which can be poured at will as if from a bottle. When they relax at the end of the day, they have earned the right to do so. Otherwise they are more disciplined than airline pilots. Significantly, Stainton Forrest, the cleaner of Fournier Street and the Bank of England, told me, 'A lot of people would like to be like George – he lets himself go, but afterwards he never talks about it, never says "I feel like a drink" on the day after. When he's out – *yes!* He's got so much control.'

Quite simply, Gilbert & George do not waste their time. Not once in Moscow did I hear them complain or mention a hangover. Each morning they reappeared as immaculate as if they had been put away for the night in a cupboard and just removed, dusted down by Stainton.

One of the pleasant discoveries in Moscow was the discovery of how much they have in common, yet how individual they are, as complementary as bacon is to eggs. Stiff on the first impression, they soon reveal a cosiness which tempts you to confide your innermost secrets – they would make superb if unorthodox interrogators. Gilbert appeared to be content to stay in the background, but this proved misleading. He has one of the quickest brains I know, unlike any Italian I've met, though he insists he is not really Italian, coming as he does from the Dolomites. Telling him about my early work in television, I swanked that I created a precedent by not sticking to a list of pre-prepared questions. 'But you've come to *us* with a list of questions!' he exclaimed – his sentences invariably end with an upward exclamation mark. I tried to explain that this was different, but he caught me off guard. Another time, Gilbert reminded me that I had attacked their prominence in the Royal Academy's exhibition of British Art in the Twentieth Century in my column in *Sunday Today*.

'Good lord, I'd clean forgotten. Before I met you.' I felt myself blushing, while Gilbert smiled with the satisfaction of having caught me out again.

George, who looks impassively manic – if such a look is possible – behind his specs when he poses for the camera, is transformed on his evenings off, like a Mr Pickwick on the rampage, or a kindly Mr Hyde.

They enjoy their success without dwelling on it. I have never heard them boast, but their pictures fetch increasingly high prices, especially since their visit to Moscow. At Christie's in New York, *Finding God* (1982) fetched $198,000; in November 1989, *Stepping* (1983) $165,000. The d'Offay Gallery tells me another picture sold for around $300,000 but was unable to reveal the name of the buyer. Gilbert & George seem uninterested in prices, and rightly disapproving: 'For the last five years the collectors have taken away the meaning of art by turning it into envy. The young people here in Moscow have no idea of the prices.' They admit to being pleased that the Tate Gallery bought *Death, Hope, Life, Fear* in 1989 shortly after Nicholas Serota became the new and innovative director. A supporter of their work, Serota showed Gilbert &

WHO ARE GILBERT & GEORGE?

George's travelling exhibition at the Whitechapel in 1981, before he dragged the Tate into the twentieth century.

Gilbert & George's personal art collection increases in value though it was not conceived as an investment. They had the foresight to buy early pottery made by Brannam in Barnstaple in the last century, and the work of Christopher Dresser long before his current revival. They showed me around with understandable pride, telling me about Dresser, of whom I knew nothing, though I have tried to correct this since. Gilbert & George had the wit to recognise that Dresser was the originator of the modern movement, not only before Mackintosh, before Bauhaus, and before Tiffany, but was equally good and often better – and is still more modern than most of the designer crap we have today.

Gilbert & George may not have a kitchen or a refrigerator; though they must have something to heat the coffee we drank in the room surrounded by neo-gothic vases while we discussed work. After we had been to Moscow, in the Indian summer of 1990, we sat in the small backyard with only an outdoor bench by Dresser for decoration, with a fig tree in the garden on one side, and the spire of Spitalfields rising above the rooftops on the other, against a still, blue sky that looked as if the white clouds were being pulled across it. The four bottles of Veuve Clicquot we consumed were tastier for being served at room temperature, instead of being plucked from a freezing fridge.

'Why were you so keen to exhibit in Moscow?'

'To test our theory of art for all; that our pictures can speak regardless of age, class and background.' 'Shake the natives – we wanted to see the response. We very much like to terrorise our viewers and make them think anew.'

'Has it changed you in any way?' For once they hesitated.

'No,' said George, 'we did it.' Gilbert added, 'Maybe we're more cynical. It was a great experience.' George concluded, 'It feels different having such a show behind us.'

WHAT KEEPS YOU AWAKE AT NIGHTS? Sexual fantasies

WHAT OBJECTS DO YOU ALWAYS CARRY WITH YOU? Contraceptives

CHAPTER FOUR

WHY THE HATRED?

I would rather see a recognisable doodle by John than the squiggly lines of Bridget Riley, the dripping paint thrown by Bruce McLean at his canvas, the photographic collage by Gilbert & George, aptly entitled *Wanker*, or the black square which passes for a picture by Bob Law in 1977, *Bordeaux Black Blue Black*.

Daniel Farson, *Sunday Today*, 18 January 1987

(On the exclusion of Augustus John from the exhibition of British Art in the Twentieth Century)

At this stage I knew little of Gilbert & George's work apart from its reproduction. Ignorance is no excuse for the philistine and today these same pictures with their wilfully provocative titles – *Wanker*, *Prick Ass*, *Bummed* and *Smash the Reds* – interest me as examples of their early photo-collages of lost youths who scrawl their way through the decaying background of East London like the hurt graffiti on the walls behind them. This has been interpreted as an indictment of Britain today.

Nor had I seen the work which first brought them to the notice of the public when they performed their Living Sculpture in 1970 with *Underneath the Arches*, their most popular presentation, followed by the *The Red Sculpture*, when they painted themselves red.

Altogether there were 56 such presentations with Gilbert & George appearing at the Royal College of Art with Bruce McLean; in Bromley having a meal with David Hockney; and venturing further afield to Berlin, Turin, Oslo, Lucerne, Rome, Sydney, Melbourne, Tokyo and New York, between 1968 and 1977.

QUEER, 1977. 300 x 250 cm.

WHY THE HATRED?

The closest I came to seeing Gilbert & George's Living Sculpture was at the Groucho Club late one night in the September following our return from Moscow. A florid new pianist was trilling at the upright and George, in the best of spirits, went over to talk to him. He came back delighted. 'He's going to play *Underneath the Arches*!'

'No!' I exclaimed. 'There's no chance ... you wouldn't perform, would you?'

'Of course,' said George, beaming.

And then the pianist came over and said he had forgotten how to play it after all.

Though Gilbert & George had told me about their Living Sculpture, which came about when they were broke and could not afford painting materials or a studio, I had never seen them perform. So I asked George Melly for his first-hand experience.

'I can't remember exactly when I first saw Gilbert & George,' he wrote to me, 'but my children, although small, were big enough to take along on my second visit so I'd guess it to be towards the end of the Sixties. I remember *where* it was, a small upstairs gallery in Glebe Place, Chelsea, and possibly Nigel Greenwood was the entrepreneur. Greenwood, later the Diaghilev of minimalism, told me to go and see them in the first place.

'In the otherwise empty room was a platform table, a wind-up gramophone, and Gilbert & George. Dressed in drab brown suits, they wore gloves and had gilded their faces. They moved like automata, jerkily as though programmed. They may have had rolled umbrellas. On the gramophone was Flanagan and Allen singing *Underneath the Arches* – I'm pretty sure it was a gramophone and not a tape because I seem to remember either Gilbert or George winding it up. Actually, Gilbert & George themselves sang the purely orchestral verse, but mimed to Flanagan and Allen singing the chorus. For this they stood on the table moving jerkily to the music. It was an absurd and touching spectacle.

'What was most impressive about it, though, was that they started this three-minute routine at, I think, nine or ten am, and continued until six pm with no variations whatsoever. I became mildly obsessed with them, but however quietly I crept up the stairs they were always at it. I think it lasted for several weeks – certainly a week. They never showed any reaction to the presence of the public but if you were there at the end (I never was) I believe they offered you a sherry. I brought the children over from NW6 in a taxi. The taxi-man, at my suggestion, came up to see them. "They've got to be fucking barmy" was his reaction. I also told Michael Astor about them at a dinner party he gave in the neighbourhood. He went to see them the next day and became almost as obsessed as I.'

Afterwards, George Melly followed their progress with interest. He heard they appeared as Living Sculpture at the Rolling Stones concert in Hyde Park after the death of Brian Jones, and he received 'beautifully printed little cards in various colours with statements on them like "To be with art is all we need", and later another series about them getting methodically drunk on different drinks. There was also an invitation to attend or rather witness a dinner party at which they were hosts to David Hockney. It was somewhere in the suburbs and alas I declined. It was printed on a carefully mottled paper. I later saw an exhibition of huge pencil drawings of themselves in country landscapes – clumsy, scribbly, and rather endearing.

'I heard that one of them was coshed unconscious by some skin-heads in the East End, and the other sat by the bed equally, if voluntarily, immobile, until his friend recovered.'

Plainly, Gilbert & George's performance sculpture had a wistful innocence which appealed to George Melly's sense of the absurd. There was nothing to find fault with. Yet, as with so many, he cannot accept them in the same way now, disliking their 'rigid formula, which I find boring and predictable, and their imagery'.

'They proclaim to be little Englanders, strange considering one is Italian, and speak like caricatures of old and particularly reactionary Colonels. I've no objection to them being gay or fancying skinheads, but they elevate these same wog- and gay-bashing yobs into heroes. Nor am I impressed or shocked by the graffiti, shit, spunk etc in their work, but I am repelled by such symbols as a severed black head. Their own obsessions are their business, but I don't see why I should applaud them for holding them. I find the stained glass window formula increasingly empty. I see why they're popular. You can tell a Gilbert & George work at 100 paces or more and the rich, who collect, want their acquisitions to be recognised immediately, and Gilbert & George certainly fit *that* bill. But I see no development, no "good" or "bad" examples of their work, simply the appreciation of a rigid system. How serious are they? How much do they mean what they transmit? I neither know nor care. Their recent and generous contribution to AIDS research I applaud. Otherwise I simply regret their gradual ossification from merry pranks to tendentious and predictable fossils.'

Melly's disillusionment is shared by most art critics and 'experts' – though they may not have appreciated the Living Sculpture in the first

THE SINGING SCULPTURE, 1970. Nigel Greenwood Gallery, London.

place. When I chose two of their works for *Gallery* I did so in the knowledge that they would arouse controversy, though I did not expect the antagonism to be so general.

There seems to be difficulty in separating the art from the artist: show a Bacon or an Auerbach and the panellists talk about the painting; show a Gilbert & George and they talk of Gilbert & George. Admittedly Gilbert & George have brought this on themselves by turning their lives into art, but such judgement inevitably smacks of ignorance, for they are rarely what they seem.

'I imagine they're two very dull people,' said the writer Paul Bailey as *Jungled* came on the screen, 'less than meets the eye.' Which shows that he does not know them. In this respect, Gilbert & George are willing victims of their own deception.

Frank Whitford, an art historian who appears regularly on *Gallery* and whose knowledge of art astounds the other contestants, wrote to me that he enjoyed interviewing them for BBC Radio though he realised afterwards that they had revealed nothing about themselves. 'They reminded me of actors in a two-handed play with everything so well rehearsed that it didn't matter what questions were asked. Only after the interview was over and they were showing me their collection of pots and furniture did they become relatively normal conversation partners: engaged, enthusiastic, genuine. I did, however, get the impression that they are absolutely genuine in their art, genuine above all in their desire to use it to control the feelings of those who look at it. They want to annoy and disgust as well as to amuse and entertain, and it's almost impossible to make art that does this any more. I don't think they're intellectually very sound, but they are enormously clever.'

He echoed the widespread curiosity over what they are really like. 'Their greatest achievement is to create the (possibly accurate) image that they have no life outside their art. No one, not even their assistants, ever sees them relaxing or behaving conventionally. No one has any idea of what they do when they get up in the morning, how they seem when they watch television, whether they've ever been ill, how they act when they're with their mothers, etc. Can you imagine them even going to the lavatory or having a bath? They seem to live out all the time totally artificial lives and have lived them for so long that they seem incapable of responding spontaneously to anything.'

That, of course, is exactly the mysterious impression they wish to give. Knowing them, this isolation is not the whole truth. They surprise me constantly with references to a television programme or articles I have written in such diverse newspapers as the *Daily Telegraph* or *The European*, revealing an awareness of what is going on outside their private world.

Frank Whitford detected a significant truth which escapes most of the critics: 'They're so anxious to stress how much hostility their work arouses. They gloss over the fact that more than half the most widely read critics and almost all the big museum people aren't hostile at all. On the contrary. And the irony is that those who are most hostile are precisely the kind of "ordinary" people who Gilbert & George claim are all for them and for whom, they claim, their work is primarily intended.'

I am not sure about the so-called 'ordinary people', but this is true of the critics as I discovered when I sorted through their formidable array of press cuttings, and the reviews of previous shows, particularly the Hayward in 1987.

Eminent critics like Marina Vaizey may not *like* their work but do recognise its power. 'On the evidence of their career to date Gilbert & George are among the most disturbing artists at work anywhere since the war' (*Sunday Times*, 12 July 1987).

Polly Devlin expressed a common feminine (and feminist) reaction in *International Herald Tribune* when she complained, 'Everything that is ordinarily human and womanly in me bewails this exhibition.' Yet she started her review: 'When one walks into the Gilbert & George show at the Hayward Gallery, one is filled with dread and alarm. For to enter these big rooms full of light streaming, as it were, through stained glass, is like entering a cathedral. Instead, we find here an anti-cathedral, a temple to the profane and even to the damned, and the responses go on to red alert.'

Other critics hedge their bets with humour: 'In some respects,' wrote William Feaver in the *Observer*, 'Baden-Powell would have thoroughly approved of the way Gilbert & George conduct themselves pictorially. He'd have liked the manliness, the blatant piety, the evident reverence for national institutions, the lack of female interest and the ability of the pair of them to get the lads eating, so to speak, out of their hand. With any luck he wouldn't have noticed the occasional turd or worse.' (Lord Baden-Powell founded the British Boy Scouts.) Yet Feaver concedes, 'The impact is heraldic but the demeanour is epic, for even in this clutter of selves you become prepared to accept that Gilbert & George are bringers of momentous tidings.'

This proves that the condemnation is not so universal as Gilbert & George would like us to believe. Yet it is undeniable that they are reviled to an unparalleled extent; indeed the antipathy towards them personally is so unrelenting that many people will dislike the idea of this book and condemn it unread because it deals with Gilbert & George.

In the opinion of Sir Alfred Munnings, Picasso deserved to be booted down the stairs, and he tried to have Stanley Spencer arrested on a charge of obscenity. The Churchills burnt Sutherland's portrait of Sir Winston.

Most worthwhile artists are reviled in their time; even Monet's paintings enraged a venerable art critic who attached the word 'Impressionism' as a term of derision. Invective is a healthy part of criticism, yet I can think of no other contemporary artist who has received such bile as Gilbert & George.

Waldemar Januszczak, the art critic for the *Guardian* and subsequently Commissioning Arts Editor for Channel 4, is an interesting case in point. I would expect him to be unsympathetic to Gilbert & George's right-wing stance and his dislike was obvious when he paid a visit to

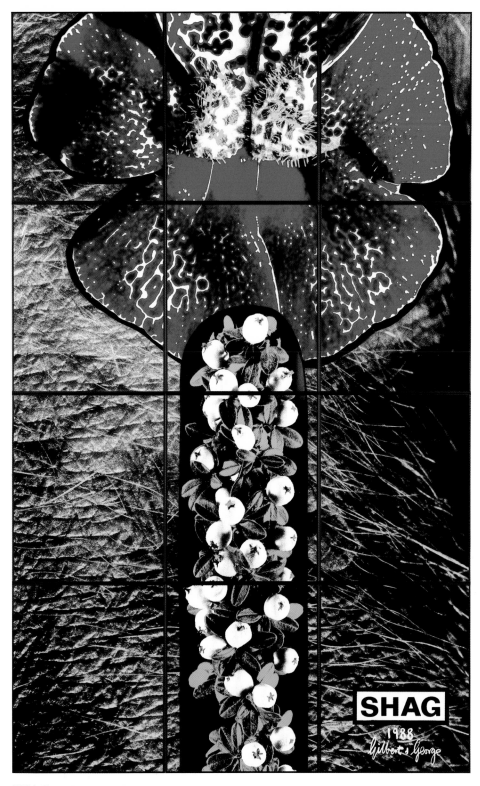

SHAG, 1988. 241x151 cm.

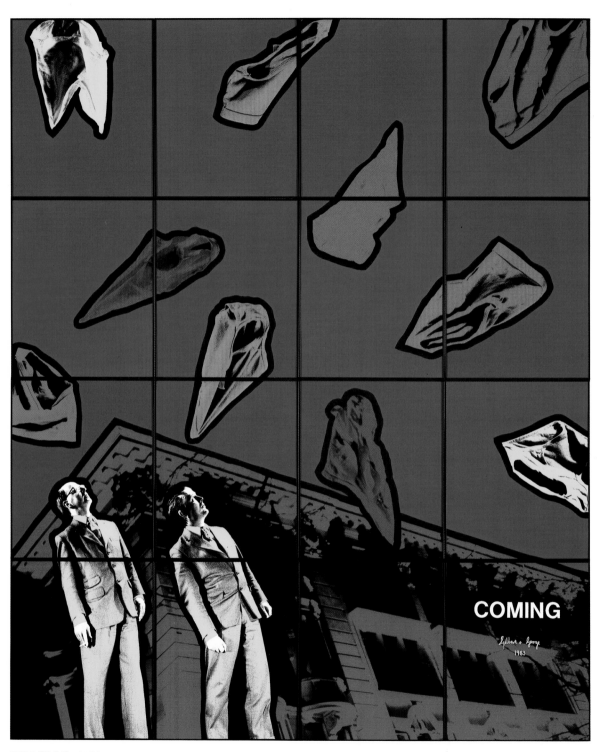

COMING, 1983. 241x201 cm.

LONE, 1988. 241x201 cm.

MAY MAN, 1986. 241x250 cm.

THE VIEWER, 1988. 241x250 cm.

THE EDGE, 1988. 241x201 cm.

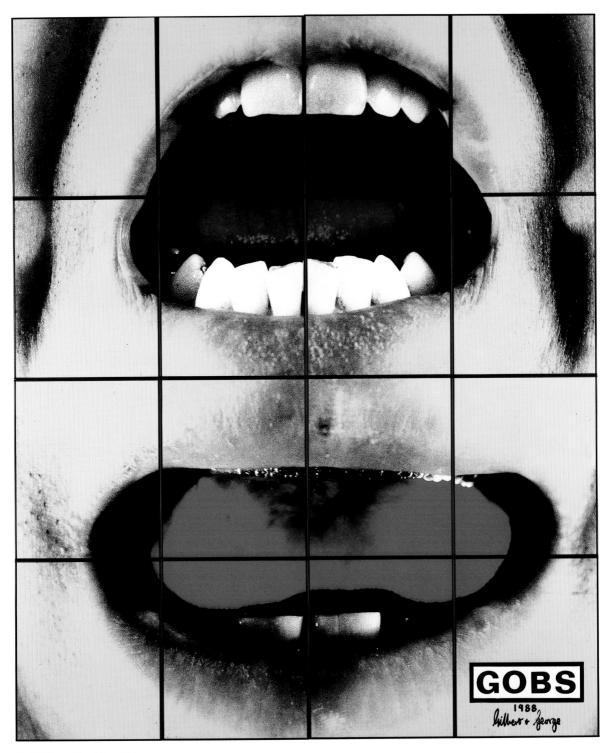

GOBS, 1988. 241x201 cm.

SEE, 1987. 241x451 cm.

HERE, 1987. 302 x 351 cm.

FLOW,1988. 253 x 284 cm.

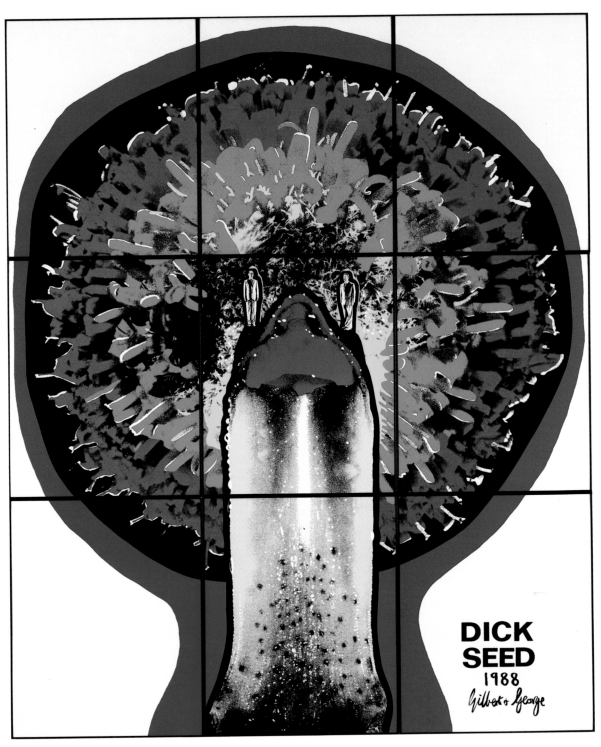

DICK SEED, 1988, 226 x 190 cm.

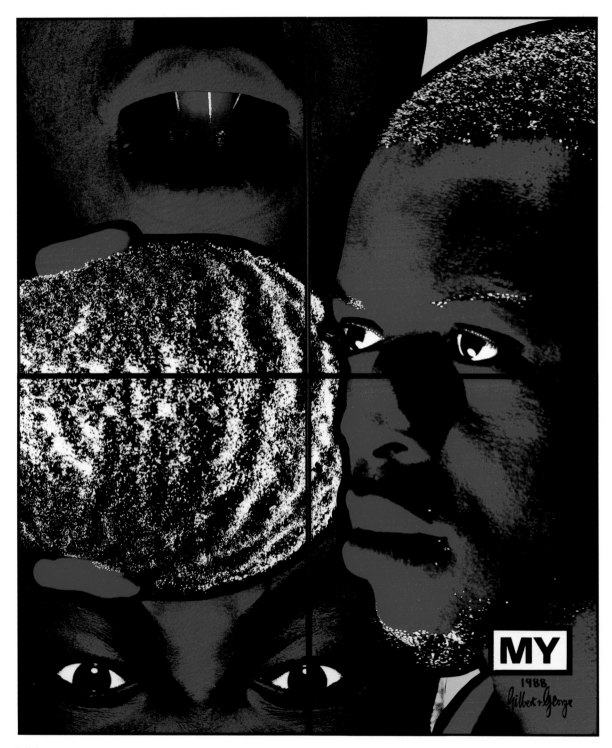

MY, 1988. 169x142 cm.

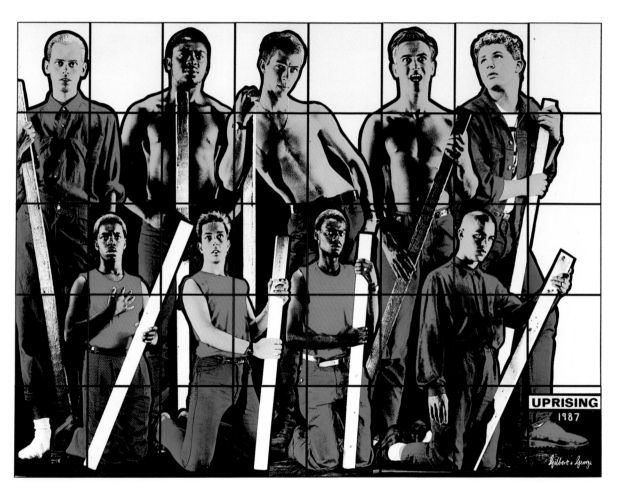

UPRISING, 1987. 302 x 401 cm.

LANDER, 1988. 181x250 cm.

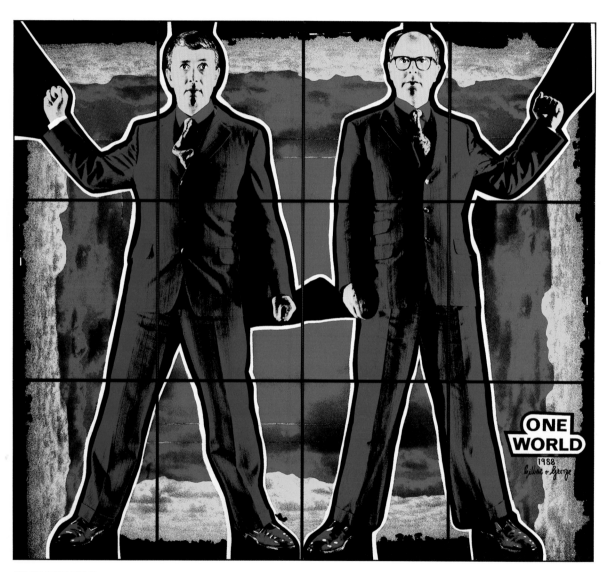

ONE WORLD, 1988. 226 x 254 cm.

GEORGE THE CUNT AND GILBERT THE SHIT, 1970. A magazine sculpture.

Fournier Street in 1984, 'Determined not to play the game, i.e. determined not to forget that I was taking tea with living people rather than the self-styled "living sculptures".' They were at loggerheads from the 'off', especially when Waldemar referred to the popularity of the Picasso show at the Hayward:

> At my mention of Picasso, George nearly bursts a blood vessel in his domed forehead and Gilbert chokes on his monosyllables. I am informed that the name of that 'foreign dago wanker' is never to be mentioned in this house. Forced to play the game I mention Picasso's name as often as I can for the remainder of the conversation.

> It cannot have been easy being Gilbert & George over the past fifteen years. The shouts of 'filthy queers' must have hurt. So has the lack of official acceptance which they complain of incessantly, although here their self-pity is harder to stomach. They've made a lot of money. They hang in the Tate. The international art world fawns over them. What more do they want?

WHY THE HATRED?

They can never speak directly to the working-class yobs who are the object of their paedophile fantasies in their work. They will never be taken to the hearts of the right-wing buffoons they identify with so theatrically in their politics. Buffoons hate queers as much as they hate Pakis.

Giles Auty, the art critic for the *Spectator*, has no time for them, asking, 'Can one sensibly question any calamities that befall a society which makes Gilbert & George into cultural heroes?' (29 April 1989). Auty even cast doubt on their motives in donating the proceeds of their 1989 d'Offay exhibition to AIDS research: 'A number of notices which have already appeared suggest to me that reviewers, acting in a similar spirit of benevolence, have waived their rights to critical comment.' This surely verges on paranoia.

For an assault really under the belt you need to turn to Brian Sewell who attacked them in the *Standard* under the headline BEWARE OF STRANGE MEN WHO DO FUNNY THINGS.

Surprisingly, Sewell concentrates on the rumours surrounding their private lives. As these have never been denied, they remain no more than rumours, but he exploits them to his advantage: 'Think of a dirty word for a sexual act, a body function, or a genital part, and you may well find it incorporated in the photo-constructions of Gilbert & George. In 1977 they had a binge of bollocks, bums and buggers (their words, not mine), and then went off the boil into what they conceived as modern moralities, with only occasional lapses into the lavatorial vernacular of the Army.'

Sewell's sense of outrage seems genuine. He is justified in believing 'pornography is a private preserve, a matter for personal decisions, and I do not want the catalogue of Gilbert & George to poke my nose into the cleft between anyone's parted buttocks, and least of all into a sphincter so relaxed that its proper place is in a textbook of medical mysteries.' He is unjustified in making his conclusion: 'I understand that Gilbert & George find their subjects in the streets of Spitalfields – local colour, so to speak; imagine the youngster taken home and undressed, Gilbert & George giving their directions from under the black cloth (their photography is dismally old-fashioned and stagy); what must he think of these two artists getting away with the very contact against which he must at one stage have been warned (beware of strange men who ask you to do funny things) simply because they proclaim it art and not pornography?'

This is nasty stuff, inviting if not inciting Lynch's law. He accuses Gilbert & George of 'taking the charlatan's way out' but the pity is that he consistently despoils his own talent by resorting to popular abuse. Not only should he know better – he *does*.

The persistent vendetta on the part of Peter Fuller is less easy to dismiss. Fuller was the art critic for the *Sunday Telegraph* and the founder and editor of *Modern Painters* (named after his admiration for Ruskin), one of the most brilliant art magazines ever published. Peter Fuller himself was an interesting man whose cautious, schoolboy looks belied the ferocity of his views, and I was delighted when he accepted my invitation to appear on *Gallery*, for this gave me the chance to meet him in Bristol where HTV filmed the programme late in 1989, for transmission in 1990. In spite of his daunting reputation, I believed that I would find him sympathetic and this proved to be the case. In the course of the afternoon as we killed time before the first rehearsal, we spoke generally and I referred to his vendetta against Gilbert & George in particular. He admitted that he felt a genuine hatred towards them.

This had been evident in Roger Scruton's 'Beastly Bad Taste' in one of the early issues of *Modern Painters* which set the tone for the subsequent attacks:

> Their work, it could hardly be called art, is easy to understand for the simple reason that it contains nothing to understand.

> Their titles are lifted from the gutter – 'two cocks', 'tongue fuck cocks', 'friendship pissing', 'shit faith' and the like – while the images fail to be disgusting only because Gilbert & George are so devoid of artistic talent as to be capable of producing no emotion whatsoever. They have little understanding of surface or light; their colours are those of the playground and the supermarket, and their lines are executed either photographically or in the hard-edged manner of the comic strip.

This attack on their technique is curious – what is so wrong with the colours of the playground or the hard-edged manner of the comic strip? That is how they work. Then Roger Scruton condemned their work on a higher level altogether:

> Where there is an absence of beauty, impossibility of beauty, the overthrow of beauty's empire, there Gilbert & George stand drivelling their ritual paean of the beautiful, uttering the word in the same tone of voice as they utter 'shit', 'fuck', 'cock' and 'buggery'.

WHY THE HATRED?

Roger Scruton concluded with a statement on the function of art today which was so impassioned that it commands respect:

> A work can now perform its economic function without being loved or admired; nobody need be awakened by it or moved by its deeper meaning. The money pours through it unresisted, like sewerage through a drain, and the civilising function of art – the function which justified all this extravagance and caused the patron to benefit from his purchase as much as the artist from the sale of it – has been finally set aside.

This is an extraordinary statement. In effect Gilbert & George are indicted as the murderers of all that is good in modern art. Peter Fuller followed this up with his own review of the d'Offay exhibition in April 1989 under the heading THE EVIL OF BANALITY. 'But life *is* banal!' Gilbert remarked to me in Moscow. Fuller described the show as the 'tackiest' he had seen in London for two decades and took exception to the book by Wolf Jahn:

> It was, of course, Hannah Arendt who first used the phrase 'the banality of evil' after observing the Nazi war criminals in the dock at Nuremberg; but Gilbert & George's lives and work testify rather to the evil of banality. This was brought home to me when I read a new book about the egregious pair by a little-known German writer, Wolf Jahn.

> Although *The Art of Gilbert & George*, published by Thames and Hudson at £12.95, carries no health warning, it is, in fact, a piece of 'vanity' publishing by the 'artists' themselves. (It is only because Gilbert & George have poured money into the book that such a large and lavish volume of well over 500 pages, many in full colour, can be offered to the public at this price.)

This is correct. Gilbert & George make no attempt to conceal such investments in order to promote their work and reach as wide a public as possible. Gilbert has pointed out the hypocrisy of commercial firms like British Petroleum sponsoring the catalogues and exhibitions at our leading galleries (BP sponsored the Royal Academy's British Art in the Twentieth Century) which is perfectly acceptable, yet if the artists do this themselves it is frowned upon.

Peter Fuller continued with his objection:

WHY THE HATRED?

Wolf Jahn is not an independent critic at all, but rather a hand-picked publicist: and his account of the gospel according to St Gilbert and St George makes pretty sick reading. Without any sense of irony, Jahn argues that the 'existential aesthetic' of Gilbert & George ... is 'analogous to ... the primordial divine sacrifice' of Jesus.

In fairness to Gilbert & George I should add that I have never heard them speak like this themselves and should have deflected such pomposity if I had. They can hardly be held responsible for what others write about them, though Fuller suggests that they can:

> If Jahn's book was in any way serious, it would pose a graver affront to Christian believers than ever Salman Rushdie directed towards those of the Islamic faith. As it is, however, the only interesting question raised by *The Art of Gilbert & George* is why Thames and Hudson – perhaps the best publisher of fine art books in this country – allowed themselves to be drawn into an association with such an obscene and blasphemous piece of self-promotion. Money, one can only suppose, has spoken.

Ah, money! Strange how bitter critics can become when they smell the scent of commercial success. Brian Sewell finished his diatribe in the *Standard* with a similar accusation: 'They have their paws in a crock of gold, and they will do anything to hold on to it.'

Yet Gilbert & George were offered a large sum of money in September 1990 to appear in a television commercial. I believe they were asked to advertise a car in a situation that was not belittling but neither was it typical or humorous.

'What do you think we should do?' they asked me, mentioning an astronomical figure.

'Turn it down,' I said decisively.

'We already have,' they smiled. 'We wanted to hear what you'd say.'

In a similar way, they are accused of courting publicity.

'Why on earth did you appear on *Wogan* [when Jonathan Ross took over],' a stranger asked George when he was on holiday in Torquay and ordered a drink in a pub.

'Why not?' George replied.

'Because it's beneath your dignity.'

'That's exactly why we appeared!'

WHY THE HATRED?

Ultimately, I agree with Christopher Cook who chaired a BBC *Critics' Forum* on Radio 3 (5 September 1987) and defended Gilbert & George throughout against the usual invective, rejecting the 'fascist' slur as 'a very dangerous term to use about them', preferring a 'Boy's Own hero-worship'. As the chairman, Cook had the last word: 'I think in conclusion that perhaps you're all taking them too seriously but not seriously enough.'

That is the best summing-up I have heard.

People will consider it either strong-minded or disgraceful that Gilbert & George show no forgiveness for their critics. Answering the questionnaire in the *Sunday Correspondent Magazine* in September 1990 they were asked 'Which living persons do you most despise?'

They answered: Brian Sewell; Peter Fuller [when the questionnaire was published by the *Sunday Correspondent* on 23 September 1990, Peter Fuller's name had been removed through the tact of the editor rather than the artists themselves]; and Waldemar Januszczak. I pointed out that Peter Fuller had been killed since they wrote that.

'So ...?' said George. 'Death doesn't stop one from hating someone.'

CHAPTER FIVE

THE CHAMPION –

RICHARD DORMENT

Shortly after joining the *Daily Telegraph* as the art critic, Richard Dorment discovered how risky it could be to champion the art of Gilbert & George in a conservative newspaper.

On Thursday 9 July 1987, Richard Dorment devoted half a page to their exhibition at the Hayward Gallery under the headline GILBERT & GEORGE TILL DEATH DO US PART. Unlike the majority of critics who tend to be snide even when they yield begrudging praise, Dorment had no hesitation in acclaiming them as 'part of a uniquely English tradition' comparable to Sickert with his affection for the slums of Camden Town and old Music Hall:

> Although, like artistic dandies from Whistler to Dali, they cultivate a highly controlled and mannered public image, the themes of their assemblages have been preoccupied with the very opposite of control, being about sex, boredom, loneliness, madness and death. Gilbert & George are poets who use everything that happens in their lives as material for their art. They insist that *all* their feelings and thoughts are legitimate subjects for sculpture, no matter how embarrassing for them to reveal or for us to see.
>
> They are deeply disliked by many critics because they omit the element of self-editing that most people automatically incorporate into their lives.

Richard Dorment concluded by suggesting that each individual sculpture, or picture, is only a fragment of 'an immeasurably huge mosaic' that they are still putting together.

> This will be finished only when they die. Because their art is
> about their own lives, the whole of their work is greater and
> more interesting than the parts. In some respects, the only way
> to see Gilbert & George is in these large retrospectives, which
> are, in some senses, a single work of art.

I felt this myself when I saw the Moscow exhibition in its entirety. Their
pictures impressed me individually when I saw them at the Whitworth in
Manchester, or in Aberdeen, but the impact of an exhibition is overwhelming.

Dorment's was a rare championship indeed. The following day in
the *Telegraph*'s Sixth Column, Martyn Harris aired a different view
which came close to exposing the paper's new art critic to ridicule. IT'S A
JOKE BUT AT WHOSE EXPENSE? was the heading, with the subheading:
'Controversial artists Gilbert & George are now attracting critical
acclaim including that of our own art critic. Martyn Harris thinks the art
world has been taken in.'

> They are, in fact, an enormous joke at the expense of the art
> world. They have become hugely famous in the twin citadels
> of pretension and credulity – the French and American art
> markets – and are now winning grudging acclaim from British
> art critics who have looked at them aghast for the past decade,
> hoping they might go away.

'When I read that attack I realised for the first time just how important
Gilbert & George were. Only the most powerful and subversive art can
provoke that kind of reaction,' Richard Dorment told me this in his
comfortable house in Little Venice where he lives with his family – his
wife is the novelist and reviewer Harriet Waugh. He had declined to
appear on *Gallery* which made me all the keener to meet him. Also, his
support of Gilbert & George makes him exceptional and he had expressed a willingness, even an eagerness, to talk to me about them, which
could lead to a greater understanding of their work.

He is an American, which might have something to do with it. 'It's
much harder for the British to understand Gilbert & George,' he told
me, 'than the Russians.' He could well have added 'and the Americans
too'.

'They hit a nerve in England. They do not paint what the British
want to see, still less what they want to believe, about their country.
They tell the truth. That is why foreigners love them and they are so
vilified at home. What other British artists treat such subjects as the

filthiness of London, alcoholism, AIDS, and racial hatred on the one hand,' asked Dorment, 'and on the other the grandeur and beauty of a city in decline? They rarely do a piece that is entirely one-sided. If their subject is London they will include the glories of its architecture, but also the dog shit in the streets.'

Richard Dorment is red-haired, which suits his temperament, alert and energetic, speaking rapidly as he stressed that artists should not be confused with their work. 'To take a random example: though of course he is a much less political and far less controversial figure, Howard Hodgkin the man is never confused with Hodgkin the artist. If he is criticised at all, it is as a painter. Gilbert & George are always attacked as individuals, as if what they do and who they are were the same thing.'

When I suggested that they encourage this personal identification with their work to a calculated extent, Richard Dorment explained that the 'façade' of their clothing and public personas parodied and paid tribute to the great English middle classes. 'A good comparison would be to T.S. Eliot who wrote his most passionate poetry after assuming the bland appearance of a bowler-hatted bank clerk. They are the English "everyman". In that guise they are able to express the lower-middle-class, *Daily Mail*-reading point of view. Remember that these are two *artists*. Like novelists, they have invented two characters who can speak for them. Through Gilbert & George they can say anything they want to say. It allows them to be outrageous and make points which other British artists and writers dare not mention. Part of the hatred they generate has to do with saying things that are unsayable. As a result, they're hated both by left-wing *and* right-wing critics.'

I mentioned the opposition from the critic Peter Fuller. 'Ironically, of all critics Peter Fuller had the most in common with Gilbert & George. He was all for returning humanist content into contemporary art. It was very strange to me that he appeared not to understand that in addition to the strong visual punch the AIDS paintings carried, they were all about death, grief, love and fear. It was all terribly moving, and yet Peter couldn't get beyond the titles, which he claimed shocked him.'

As for the nagging criticism that Gilbert & George are merely technique: 'It's very arduous and complicated, and the effects they produce are spectacular. Photography is used as part of the process of what they do, but they are anything but photographers. By removing all traces of their own hand from the production of a piece, they achieved a unique effect that is somewhat akin to Pop Art's use of slick advertising imagery. This puts a barrier between the viewer and the often ferociously strong content in their paintings. Remember that for many years they described what they did as "sculpture", not painting.

'The real comparison: they are the successors to, but much greater than, Francis Bacon. Francis Bacon is able to express his own predicament; Gilbert & George can do that but go much further, beyond the self-obsessed private world of Bacon's paintings which are in a certain sense self-portraits. By using symbols of Britain, they go beyond their own predicament. One feels one knows a lot about Francis Bacon but not Gilbert & George. They've achieved a device which allows them to express universal subjects; their art has developed in a most extraordinary way, as Francis Bacon's never has.'

Richard Dorment returned to his comparison with Walter Sickert and his interest in the Camden Town murders and London music halls, echoed in Gilbert & George's Living Sculpture *Underneath the Arches*. 'Sickert used the underbelly of British life and Gilbert & George are in an equally intense British tradition. They began as performance artists and I don't think they've stopped.'

To explain the hatred felt towards them, I raised the inevitable bugbear – boys. 'As an art historian, I have to answer to that. Ever since the Renaissance the Apollo Belvedere has been the West's ideal of male beauty. Look at the scrawny, pot-bellied kids in Gilbert & George. Hardly heroic specimens. I am sure they are deliberately repellent, evoking the First War scandal when so many conscripts were revealed as shockingly undernourished. I think they're saying something about Britain. If they were fascist they'd find better specimens than these – hardly Nordic – nor erotic. More telling of the truth – this is British youth today. Their critics say that a youth waving a flag must be a skinhead or a fascist – I don't see it that way. Gilbert & George's pictures never mean one particular thing. There is room in every Gilbert & George for interpretation; they don't slam you on the head. There is room for individual response and you find new things in them all the time.'

I asked about his claim that they will be remembered in 100 years' time. 'Oh yes! More than Francis Bacon. They belong to the Northern tradition that includes Brueghel – Munch – Otto Dix – the opposite of reassurance. There are very few artists whose exhibition one wouldn't dream of missing – Gilbert & George are the exception.'

Richard Dorment made me aware, as I had not been before, of the way they reflect contemporary London and the desolation of the East End in particular. 'Their celebration of London has not been recognised; their series on the sculpture of London is one of the most beautiful

THE ALCOHOLIC, 1978. 241x201 cm.

things they have done – their East End seems to go back to Dickens and certainly to Hogarth's *Gin Lane*. They do not pretend that London's parks are leafy glens, you can sense the alienation of nature barely hanging on. They're also in the great tradition of William Blake – the visionary side – two people looking at this urban hell.'

Richard Dorment says one should not look for a single meaning in their pictures, that they show the bestial side of life as well as the exalted – the dog shit and the glory. 'Like T.S. Eliot there is a passionate poetry behind the façade – they have constructed their own *Waste Land*.'

This is a persuasive argument, for T. S. Eliot is a dandy name to bandy, and inspired Bacon's image of *Sweeney Agonistes* in 1967. But are the youths really such pathetic specimens and is the urban scene really so hellish? The youths are twee rather than erotic and do not seem undernourished, more like potential body-builders without a chance, in spite of the narcissism involved.

There are numerous 'leafy glens', as in *Lone* (1988) where a youth in pink jeans is walking across an armpit surrounded by cherry blossom, and though odd things are happening in *The Viewer* (1988) and the skyline of the Thames has the hostility of tower blocks, some people, and possibly the artists themselves, might find this beautiful. The blue in *May Man* is carried through in exactly the right places which indicates the deliberation involved, while the foliage in *Lander* and *Man-God* (both shown in Moscow) is lush.

The exception is *Here* (1987) with the two gigantic figures of Gilbert & George in blue, their palms outstretched, with an astounding panorama of Spitalfields behind them. This has the element of despair which Richard Dorment refers to, and a curiously haunting quality, yet the wretchedness of the street below is caused partly by the refuse of the market after it has closed, and all markets, be they in London, Venice or Paris, look unloved when the turmoil is over.

I needed to go back to the earlier work such as the *Dirty Words* series in 1977 to find their 'Waste Land' in the black and white bleakness where vagrants stare and shuffle and young men seem to do nothing at all. In *The Alcoholic* a dosser sprawls unconscious on a crate; *Queer* has the poignant combination of London's skyline with the street squalor below. Their work in 1980 is almost wholly photographic, though *Cemetery Youth* returns to a skilful composition of photographic collage with a row of faces at the top, apparently of the same youth, and a row of tombstones underneath.

Yet I can understand if people have doubts when confronted with this work for the first time – can this be art? A conventional reaction which underestimates the crucial role of photography in their work, which discards the brush.

A picture like *Dusty Corners* as early as 1975, when George had hair and Gilbert looked even more boyish, shows how beautiful such photographic constructions can be.

Dorment stresses, 'They're not new. They've been around since the early Seventies but recognition comes late in England – "a prophet is not without honour, save in his own country" – but within twenty years' time they'll be much loved when people actually look instead of listen. They are the most important British artists alive.'

CHAPTER SIX

A SENSE OF *DÉJÀ VU*

Due to Gilbert & George's good humour, the departure from Heathrow was painless, in contrast to the usual ordeal, with a swift ride across the Hammersmith flyover and down the motorway which was empty at seven o'clock on the Saturday morning.

I observed their discretion in the airport lounge after we checked in: no VIP treatment expected, none of the impatience or bad temper induced by airports.

I stocked up with the duty-free gifts I had been advised to bring to Russia – chocolates, plastic half-bottles of Johnny Walker, and cartons of Marlboro cigarettes, which proved the most valuable form of currency, to add to my arsenal of soap, socks and books. An elegant saleslady confronted me with a new brand of eau de cologne 'on special offer', pitching her sales talk so skilfully that I bought a box in order to please her – which proved the perfect gift in the Caucasus for Olga, the girl-friend of the sleepy-eyed student Dennis. For good measure, she threw in several samples, one of which I used in Moscow to freshen me up a few nights later, unaware that this was undiluted perfume until James Birch reeled away from me, clutching his nose.

This sophisticated woman had not heard of Gilbert & George, which disappointed though it did not surprise me. The British have little interest in their contemporary artists, and Gilbert & George were unre-cognised in the lounge except by a smartly dressed young man who asked for their autograph, which George gave with a flourish and at such length that Gilbert turned to me with a shrug of impatience. 'Oh George, he does make such a *thing* of it!' adding the single word '*Gil-bert*' before '*& George*'. The young man thanked them politely but left with no attempt at conversation, not even to ask where they were going.

Travelling Club Class, we were fuelled with gins and tonic, leaving

Stalin's immense highways add to the bleakness of Moscow. On knowing it better, I started to wander, but still found it a forbidding city.

Photo. Keith Davey.

me in such a state of euphoria that I left one of my duty-free bags in the plane when we arrived at Moscow airport. Before I could stop him, George hurried back to retrieve it, to be met by a stewardess with the carrier bag on her way to find me. I noticed that he did this instinctively without any fuss or show of irritation, which would have been wholly justified.

While Gilbert & George were swept away in a Rover 2000 (apparently one of two such cars in Russia) by the father of Sergei Klokhov, I went with James Birch and Judy Adam from the d'Offay Gallery, who had come to meet us, in the minibus which overflowed with welcoming Russians, including Sasha (short for Alexander) the driver, and Sasha Rozin, Moscow's leading art critic, a joyful, volatile personality who insisted on stopping at the first lay-by where he produced a bottle of Georgian cognac of such ferocity that it melted the paper cups, even when three were put together.

Sasha had blazed the way by proclaiming his enthusiasm for Gilbert & George's work in his magazine. 'I write that I like them for their total humanity. Not just the Russians, not Jewish, *everybody*!' This was echoed in the first of many toasts. Throughout our days in Moscow, Sasha was constantly on his feet, glass in hand, toasting the fellowship of nations, peace for mankind, wives, children, childhood friends, and Gilbert & George. Having adopted James Birch as a 'brother', Sasha had formed a Brotherhood of Humanoids and as the Russian for 'brother' is 'brat', I was embraced as a fellow 'Brat', which was better than 'Brit' which conjures up an image of a football supporter abroad, wearing union-jack shorts.

Looking at the Russian countryside and the glades of shimmering silver birch, I had the odd sensation that I had been there before. This was strengthened in Moscow with occasional, illogical echoes of a distant childhood. Mentioning this later to George – that everything was strange yet hauntingly familiar – I learnt that he felt the same, explaining it as a memory of post-war Britain at an impressionable age, when the queues, rationing, and grey austerity were as much a part of everyday life as they are today in Russia.

For me, there was the additional sentiment that my father had loved Russia deeply since his arrival in Tsarist Petrograd in 1914 where he intended to stay for three weeks selling American munitions to the Russian army, and stayed for three years frustrated by internal graft. He witnessed the Kerensky Revolution; John Reed became his closest friend; he covered the USSR as a foreign correspondent between the wars for the *Chicago Daily News*; climbed the Caucasus in 1929; and returned in the last war as war correspondent for the *Daily Mail*, cooped up with the other journalists in Kubyshev far from the front, experiencing his final and utter disillusionment with Communism.

Yet he retained his love for Russia and the Russian people from the day he set foot there, as I was starting to do in my own minuscule way in that insignificant lay-by with the irrepressible Sasha.

'Petrograd during the first years of the war,' wrote my father in his autobiography *The Way of a Transgressor*, provided the perfect life of dissipation. I'm not so sure it did not provide the perfect life all around. I know I could never have dreamed a better one. Englishmen who were born in Russia and lived there declared it was the finest life in all the world.'

Yet, as his frustration grew in the face of governmental corruption, he described a situation which was not so far removed from that in Moscow in 1990:

Then the streets of Petrograd and Moscow presented not only pitiable but frightening signs of privation and starvation. There were queues around each provision shop that sometimes encircled the whole block in which it stood. In Moscow I actually saw a boot shop that had a queue which had been standing there for days, that went twice around a large city block.

The parallels are surprisingly close. In 1914 Kerensky enjoyed greater popularity abroad than he did at home, like Gorbachev today, and trod a similar tightrope between the forces of the Left (represented by Lenin) and those of the far Right (the military) until he was toppled.

In December 1990 at least a million tons of supplies were stuck in the ports. In 1914 the distribution of food, supplies and arms was equally hopeless.

With its two mouths – Archangel and Vladivostok – choking with the food of war, Russia lay like a prostrate Mars, starving to death. It was a process of wastage that one could witness on every side. As plain as watching a man die from pthisis in a hospital ward. A man who was becoming rotten inside. The tales of high officials who had been caught and shot for corruption became more frequent every day. We lived in an atmosphere equivalent to being in a city in the last days of siege.

Plus ça change in Russia – Tsarist or Communist. Over the next few days I found the same siege mentality, and thought that Moscow was the most exciting yet saddest city I had known, with a fearful feeling of impending doom. On my last day, as I shall tell, I came face to face with Gorbachev, as my father had with Lenin when he saw him on a raised platform across the Neva:

A short dumpy figure, with an enormous dome of a head, high cheekbones giving a sinister contemptuousness to his Tartar eyes. The great Lenin! But he was not 'great' to any but a very few people then. He was just this undersized new agitator in an old double-breasted blue suit, his hands in his pockets, speaking with an entire absence of that hysterical arm-waving that so characterised all his fellow countrymen. 'Yes,' he was saying, 'it is the Capitalists and our diplomats who make the wars. Not the people. They get rich, we get killed. You left the soil and factories to work under the Capitalist system

(Sixth from right) my mother, Eve Stoker, as a young VAD nurse in the Anglo-Russian Hospital in Petrograd in 1916, with the Russian Imperial family behind her.

again – those of you who are left alive. *What do you get from war*? Wounds, suffering and death.'

During the Kerensky Revolution, John Reed told my father, 'The next time you hear the machine-guns, old boy, you put on a red necktie. It's going to be the only safe colour in Petrograd. And this time it will be a *real* revolution.' Reed had just come back from seeing Lenin for the first time, and my father said his eyes were still half-blinded, as if he had seen a vision, as if he had seen God!

My father's affinity with the Russian people was shared by my mother who sailed to Russia as a VAD nurse in January 1916 when she was eighteen years old. Though she may have passed my father along the Nevsky Prospekt, they did not meet until the war was over when my

My father in Petrograd with his fiancée, Vera Thornton, daughter of an English mill-owner whose mill was taken over by the Workers' Soviet during the Kerensky Revolution. 1917.

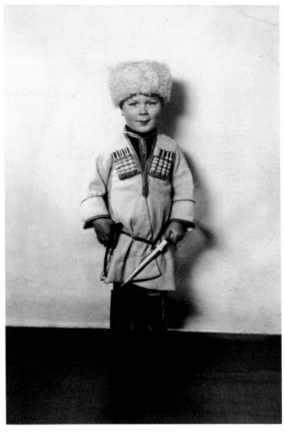

Myself in the Cossack uniform brought back by my parents after a subsequent visit to Russia.
Christmas 1930.

father was in hospital in London after crashing his plane in Egypt while serving in the Royal Canadian Flying Corps. They were introduced by friends who realised how much they had in common, and were married in the Savoy Chapel in 1920.

I possess the letters she sent to my grandmother after arriving at the Anglo-Russian Hospital that occupied the former palace of the Grand Duke Dimitri Pavlevitch.

> Well, darling, our opening is really taking place *at last* … we have had a strenuous week polishing brass and oak and cleaning marble … I watched six soldiers this morning cleaning a brass stair-rod and it gave me intense enjoyment for they look so sweet in their uniforms and have such lovely teeth and such nice names that one has to overlook the regrettable fact that

they stroll in about ten-thirty and expect heavy tips, quite irrespective of their pay, for the least service. One has the most lovely voice, and last night as I passed through the hall I heard him singing a Russian song and accompanying himself on a *balalaika*, and I wondered how many English Tommies could have done anything so good.

My mother's chattiness in her letters provides a pleasing antidote to the usual reports:

By two-thirty we were all standing in there dressed up to the nines in starched everythings, and the priests began to arrive, and dress in their wonderful gold and silver and purple clothes. Then we heard a crowd moving slowly up the stairs, and a small dowdy woman in black, like a plain edition of Alexandra – (the Empress, sister of our own Queen) but with a very sweet expression – came in and a small man in a simple khaki uniform with no orders or decorations, and very bright blue eyes that glanced from side to side – the Tsar had arrived – followed by such a crowd of gold and medals and ribbons and orders as you never saw – or certainly as I never did!!

The two little princesses, Olga and Tatiana, looked charming and so pretty in little ermine hats with white ospreys in them and little low-necked rose-coloured frocks and ermine furs and muffs. Olga is the prettiest and really lovely and all so jolly-looking and natural. All our Embassy were there in full rig and all the secretaries and Attachés we used to dance with made us roar – all covered in gold lace and things.

Later, my mother described a visit from Anastasia – 'a little girl with her hair down her back and an Alice in Wonderland comb' – and an unforgettable day when the little Czarevitch came, 'one of the most beautiful children I ever saw', and how the Russian wounded were overcome with pleasure.

I have a photograph beside me now of my mother at the feet of the Empress, described in her letter home:

We went into the big hall to be photographed and dear old Colonel Fenton, who had nearly all the medals in the world, seized me by the arm and said, '*Là – aux pieds de 'l'Imperatrice*' and pushed me down, so I have come out as large as life, leaning against her knee … the rest of us went back and had the dickens of a tea off the hired gold plate.

In contrast, another incident distressed my mother who was looking after a young man from Siberia who had to have both legs amputated and was visited by his father, a peasant who travelled nearly 1,000 miles to see his son. When he did so, with Vassili lying outside his bed with his stumps on a pillow, the old man started to shout at him, the tears pouring down his cheeks. The interpreter explained that he was *cursing* the boy – why hadn't he died? Then they would have been given a small pension – now, just look at him, a hopeless burden, another useless mouth to feed and they were nearly starving already.

One night the Grand Duke Dimitri burst into his former palace with Prince Youssoupov, both men in such a state of frenzy that the doctors assumed they were drunk as they tended to some minor cuts, until they realised they were on the verge of hysteria. That night they had killed Rasputin, though neither would say who fired the first shot after the poisoned cakes and wine had had no effect on the 'Holy Sinner' who had entranced the Tsar and Tsarina. At dawn, Dimitri fled to his estates in the Caucasus, which saved his life, and Russia was never the same, with the downfall of the Tsars as Rasputin had prophesied.

These associations enhanced my arrival in Moscow with the knowledge that both my mother and father had been there in equally traumatic times. Due to their encouragement, I studied Russian at the School of Slavonic Studies in London at the age of 16. Immersing myself in Russian films and novels, I progressed far enough to read the *Cherry Orchard* in the original – and found it hilarious – and then gave up. I arrived in Moscow with a few lingering words and two phrases, one. – 'I think you are a very wise man', and the other 'I think you are a very stupid man', hoping that I remembered them the right way round.

After checking into the Hotel Ukraine, built in Stalinist-baroque, a wedding cake with 28 storeys and no bar, I left my luggage in my surprisingly comfortable bedroom and joined the others in the ground-floor lobby we grew to know so well. Then we were driven to the home of the Union of Artists, a fine old mansion once owned by a friend of Turgenev, who had stayed there. I was photographed in the garden at the back with Gilbert & George and Judy Adam, beside more silver birch, while the atmosphere inside had the friendly informality of the Chelsea Arts Club.

By this time, euphoria had given way to drunkenness, on my part at least. It would have been remarkable otherwise, in view of British Airway's hospitality, Sasha's fiery cognac, and now his prolific toasts in vodka – you name it, we drank it. Above all, toasts to Gilbert &

It seemed an intrusion to photograph the inevitable Russian queue, for the ultimate reward in this case was a few soggy strawberries which any British shopper would reject. Yet this queue is an inescapable part of the weariness of Moscow life.   Photo. Daniel Farson.

George, which they accepted gracefully, with George murmuring, 'Very kind, very sweet, extraordinary!'

James recorded the progress of the evening in his notes: 'They like Dan for he is a good drinker. Everyone is very excited. Dan gets emotional and starts crying because there is a wedding next door. Mr Klokhov [Sergei's father] gets upset because Sasha is toasting me and not his son. Misha is upset with Richard Salmon [one of the collectors who had flown in] because he said he worked for the KGB. Afterwards Mr Klokhov insists we go to the Armand Hammer Centre which is not very nice; everyone is a bit drunk and starts dancing. Dan who already had been dancing at the wedding is now dancing with Judy Adam, and

With Gilbert & George and Judy Adam in the back garden of the Union of Artists, on our first night in Moscow.

At one of the parties given for Gilbert & George by Soviet artists: (from left to right) Mikhail Mikheyev, head of art promotion USSR's Artists' Union; James Birch; Sasha Rozin, the volatile art critic; Gilbert & George.

Photo. Daniel Farson.

(From left to right) Rudi Fuchs of the Gemeentemuseum in the Hague; James; Mikhail Mikheyev and Dolly J. Fiterman.

Misha with Sharafrat. I liked the way she showed me a photo of her parents who are dressed completely in ethnic clothes. [She had told James previously that she dared not go out on the streets at night because she came from the Republic of Azerbaijan.] George is v-drunk and keeps dropping his gin and tonics. Then everyone comes back to my room.'

I remember that wedding with the young couple so stiff and wistful that the occasion reduced me to vodka tears, with the amusing aunt who insisted we should dance. Also, dancing with Judy Adam with such abandon that my shoes split apart and had to be discarded later, which meant I had to wear my blue mountain boots reserved for the Caucasus, polishing them vigorously each morning to make them look halfway presentable, though they might have come from Lobbs as far as the ill-clad Russians were concerned.

Dancing in Russia requires no finesse but my stamina at three am astounded me until I remembered that it was only midnight by Greenwich time. However, the first of the dorm feasts in James's bedroom lingered on until I called it a day, and a night, at five o'clock and was guided down the labyrinthine corridors of the Ukraine by Misha Kurzanoff who worked for the Union of Artists and reminded George of every boy he had gone to school with. I gestured, embarrassed, at the various objects scattered on the table – the cigarettes, the whisky and the soap. 'Do, please, take whatever you like.'

Instead, Misha's eyes had fixed on my open sponge-bag and a carton of those nasty little objects which clean out one's ears, known as cotton-buds.

'Could I have these for my children?' he asked.

'Of course.' I was relieved that I had a small bag of chocolates to give them as well. I felt ashamed that I could give pleasure with something so pathetic. The embarrassment was mine alone. James told me that Misha returned to the party brandishing the cotton-buds as if they were Fabergé eggs. Even so, the discrepancy between our luxuries which we take for granted, and those of the Muscovites which scarcely exist, continues to haunt me. To photograph Gilbert & George in a queue that was waiting patiently for some squashed and soggy strawberries seemed an impertinence. To give a grown man a bar of soap, an obscenity. It is little wonder if the Muscovites are devious – 'They have to be,' said Sergei Klokhov a few nights later, 'for they have nothing.'

So ended my first day in Moscow, with an indignity of cotton-buds.

CHAPTER SEVEN

THE CATALOGUES
WEIGHED SEVEN TONS

I had no concept of the organisation needed to stage a major exhibition. It is a challenge anywhere nowadays, but in this case it was exacerbated by the problems of mounting it in Moscow.

Insurance is so prohibitive, especially since the theft in Berlin of Lucian Freud's portrait of Francis Bacon, that such exhibitions are becoming rare and, consequently, more important. Though it might be staged successfully in America, this does not necessarily mean that a show will continue to another country. Galleries and collectors are becoming possessive, understandably so when their pictures are returned in worse condition. A degree of snobbery is involved; otherwise there is little incentive to loan a picture. Lucian Freud refused to lend a painting to the second retrospective of Francis Bacon at the Tate, giving me the simple explanation that he did not like the inconvenience and boredom of strangers entering his home to remove a picture he would miss, and which might, conceivably, be damaged. Loans are no longer automatic.

The bartering involved is intricate. If a gallery possesses an outstanding example of the artist's work, the director has a certain bargaining power for transferring the show, though this proved unsuccessful in the case of the Velázquez exhibition in New York or the Van Gogh anniversary exhibition in Amsterdam, which tempted many admirers to cross the Channel but did not come to London.

In spite of such complications, the Gilbert & George exhibition proceeded smoothly, concealing the immense amount of work involved. No pictures were for sale, all were owned by individual collectors (and a few galleries) who gave their permission readily. That was the first step; then they had to be collected and brought to Moscow.

After their first visit, Gilbert & George had made a detailed maquette based on the measurements of the rooms in the New Tretyakov Gallery in the Central House of the Artists where the exhibition was being held, opposite Gorky Park. Instead of a few immense rooms, these led into each other with exciting glimpses of further pictures beyond.

Gilbert & George selected which pictures should go where, adding tiny reproductions to the maquette until the entire exhibition was complete – 'We like to have control of *everything*,' Gilbert told me emphatically.

With their emphasis on technique, the preparations for hanging are particularly important. I witnessed their concern as they saw the exhibition come to life. They knew exactly what they wanted and approached any problem head-on. 'We believe in simplicity,' said Gilbert, and this is the hardest objective to achieve. Their dedication to Moscow was absolute.

The catalogues alone cost them £60,000, translated into Russian and printed in Germany where they find the quality of reproduction superior to that in England.

Though a few pictures were flown directly to Moscow, the majority went overland in a German juggernaut. In this respect, Gilbert & George enjoyed an unusual advantage, for their photo-pieces could be dismantled and the thousands of panels transported in large wooden boxes. Even so, it was a formidable undertaking planned like a military operation: the 5,000 catalogues weighed more than seven tons. And this was apart from 32,000 postcards; stickers for taxis – a suggestion from Sergei Klokhov, which proved popular with Moscow's taxi-drivers; badges for lapels; hundreds of SHAG posters, complete with buckets, brushes and paste to stick them throughout the city; pots of paint and whitewash, with appropriate brushes, intended to brighten the gallery walls. Also, the Gilbert & George T-shirts – Russian on the front, English on the back – which were worn by young Russians of both sexes as a status symbol of supreme excellence, and comfort.

This formidable sales-force was accompanied across Europe by Paul Barratt, a young representative of the d'Offay Gallery who acted as a security guard.

PAUL'S HUNGER MARCH TO MOSCOW

Paul Barratt left London on 10 April in a Mercedes trailer with 40 works by Gilbert & George; 58 five-litre cans of white emulsion; rollers, brushes and two ladders; four Bosch drills; one crate of Bells whisky

Gilbert & George with Raymond O'Daly on their right, Paul Barratt on their left, James Birch, far right, and the Russian hanging team.

Photo. Keith Davey.

and enough food to keep the five representatives from d'Offay going for two weeks. Also, Tomas and Michael, the drivers from West Berlin who could speak no English. As Paul did not speak German, that made it quits.

When they reached Dover they had the longest clearance of the entire journey, passed by customs four and a half hours later. At ten-thirty the next morning they caught the ferry to Zeebrugge where the Germans started to drive against the clock, taking turns to sleep in the back of the cab. They reached the East-West German border at midnight and West Berlin at four-thirty. Checking into his hotel at five am, Paul slept throughout the day. The following day, as they waited for the catalogues to be delivered by the West German printers, Paul stocked up with tapes and books for company.

On Saturday they set off again, though they stopped at an East

German supermarket where Tomas bought sausages, coffee and fruit, cheaper than in the West, with the single, enigmatic word – *Poland*!

'When we crossed the Polish border I realised what they meant. My first meal was a shock. We stopped at a transport café on the road to Warsaw. We were the only vehicle in the dust-bowl carpark apart from a red Lada. Inside the car a woman exchanged money and I changed some Deutsche Marks for what seemed an enormous amount of zlotys and we went inside the "Motel", which looked like one of the cave dwellings in the *Flintstones*. Fred and Wilma were nowhere to be seen, just a rather gruesome waitress. There was no menu, you took what came with a choice of juice, tea, coffee or beer. I had coffee made from gravel ... it *was* the *Flintstones* after all. In Warsaw we stopped at another "Motel". This had no food at all. The woman at the reception desk kindly offered us some stale cake which she kept under her desk. There were no plugs or light bulbs. The following day was Easter Sunday.

'Each town we passed was celebrating. By now I was so hungry I would have gone to the communion service just to have the wafer, but we pressed on, reaching the Soviet border at three o'clock, cleared customs in half an hour and were greeted by a military officer who grinned at us revealing a mouthful of gold teeth. He was our escort to Moscow, arranged by the Union of Artists to ensure a safe passage, though it became increasingly obvious that the only accident we were likely to have would be with our escort as he bounced the few cars we came across to the sides of the road, darting forward, suddenly slowing up.

'It all became clear when he handed us over to another militia man and leant into the cab to talk to Michael. The smell of alcohol enveloped us. He was as drunk as a skunk. We got to Minsk at nine pm. There was a big party going on at the Intourist Hotel. Within ten minutes of sitting down for dinner, by now desperate to eat, I had been offered black market money, two girls, one leather jacket and a fine military watch. I stuck to the steak.'

The truck started off for Moscow at nine-thirty the next morning – 'all heavily hungover' – and reached the outskirts of Moscow at two-thirty am the following day where the militia escort left them. Paul checked into the Hotel Ukraine and reported the safe arrival of the truck to the advance party from the d'Offay Gallery which consisted of Judy Adam, the organiser of the exhibition with James Birch, and Raymond O'Daly.

Troy in Izmailovsky Park on a Saturday morning when there was a welcome show of individuality, with barbecues, a strolling jazz band of young musicians, and Gorby dolls which unfolded to reveal a smaller Brezhnev, Khrushchev, Stalin, and finally a tiny Lenin. I doubt if these are permitted today.

Photo. Daniel Farson.

94

THE CATALOGUES WEIGHED SEVEN TONS

O'DALY THE HANGMAN

Raymond O'Daly is a smiling, 28-year-old Irish-Canadian from Montreal, with the build of an ice-hockey champion and the sensitivity of a poet. He joined the d'Offay in 1984 after studying at Goldsmith's where he developed Performance Art, appearing in tableaux such as Arnolfini's Marriage with sufficient impact to be included in the Thames and Hudson book on the subject as being among the few who have proved successful in this rarefied art form. Though he joined the d'Offay as a technician, it seemed a logical progression to hang the work of Gilbert & George and he has continued to do so since Rome in 1984, with Moscow as the tenth and the most difficult exhibition.

'I wanted nine days and they gave me three, due to an unexpected exhibition of Lenin Commemorative Stamps – the most boring show I've ever seen. Then I had problems with the walls which were made of such a hard material I thought it was asbestos. Each panel had to be screwed in to the scream of drills. Gilbert & George's work is special and complicated – the Tate's picture alone consisted of 250 panels and though David Goodwin was there just to supervise and didn't have to help, he joined us in the late-night work, an absolute saint.'

TROY

As more people flew in, the Gilbert & George entourage gained an identity though it was strangely disparate, as if the cast were assembling for a large-scale musical with many contrasting parts. Troy would have played a juvenile lead. He remains an enigma. To begin with, that name – *Troy*!

In 1989 an Announcement was dropped through letter boxes with a photograph on the other side of a young man with glistening, swept-back hair and a false moustache. It stated: 'Please note that with effect from 1 July Adrian C. Price should be referred to as Troy. Please amend your records accordingly.'

Neither knowing Troy at the time nor having such records to amend, I asked why he had changed his name; after all, he could have simply dropped the 'C'.

'The decision was inspired by Greek mythology and the tale of the fall of Troy.' Before I could interrupt he forestalled me. 'This may sound pretentious to some, but this is my reasoning behind the name: I was thinking of the Trojan horse – perhaps wooden on the outside but with the power to make great changes on the inside. However, as with the great city of Troy, unless I am able to get the balance of my thought absolutely right I could fall.'

'Well…?'

'When choosing the name, I was thinking in terms of a first name, middle name and surname. For purposes of simplicity and numerological consequence I decided instead to opt for a single name.'

'I see … I *think*.' In fact I was thinking that this verged on self-indulgence when he added, deflatingly, 'I admit this has caused some confusion – the passport office said that the only similar case they encountered was with someone who changed their name to "1066".'

The astonishing thing is that Troy suits him. He is Troy. And, come to think of it again, is it odder to change your name than dye your hair red and put a stud in your nose? Just more unusual.

Without the false moustache, Troy is a smooth-faced, neat young man though enigmatic. When I asked him 'Who are you?' he shied away like a nervous animal, took control of himself, and issued another statement: 'My position is to remain in the background. Although I can assure you that once my plans are properly formulated I shall have no hesitation in going public.

'My objective is to remain pure in my sense of purpose. This may sound very Gilbert & George, something which I wouldn't deny. They have influenced my life, but not as mentors. There is little point in dwelling on the past, although it doubtless plays a major role in one's future. I changed my name to Troy not to escape the past but to make a clear separation between a life which was dictated by others, my schooling, and a life over which I assume total control. However, I am by no means a control freak! I suppose one of my very greatest drawbacks as a writer is my philosophy of preferring to withhold casting any judgement on an object or person.

'If there happens to be some form or action through which I have derived pleasure then I make an effort to introduce it to others for their interest. Gilbert & George summed it up more articulately when I first interviewed them just before their "For Aids" show at Anthony d'Offay's Gallery: "Our art is about presenting the viewer with avenues for exploration … " Art for me, is similar to history. It is not about painting some fussy picture to make a crass statement on life, which sadly is what so many misguided young artists are doing. It is about recording life, as if one was making notes in a journal.'

Troy may be suffering from an excess of the seriousness of youth,

Stainton Forrest, Gilbert & George's cleaner and friend, who attends many of their exhibitions abroad.
Photo. Daniel Farson.

DAVID ROBILLIARD, 1952–1988, Poet and Artist.   Photo. Matthew Lewis.

but that was one of the interesting things about him – that he was so thoughtful at such an early age.

Surprisingly, this was a return visit for Troy who had been to Moscow in pre-Perestroika days when Brezhnev was First Secretary and Adrian C. Price a child. I tried to find out more, but the subsequent Troy was reticent – that all belonged to his past.

THE CATALOGUES WEIGHED SEVEN TONS

This time he had been invited by Gilbert & George and the d'Offay Gallery, who paid his expenses when they learnt that he wished to cover the exhibition for *Time Out*. 'We had only met one another a year beforehand, and I think Gilbert & George took a considerable risk in believing in me.'

Stainton: Why don't the Russians like their money?
Troy: Because they haven't got any.

STAINTON FORREST

Stainton Forrest was so reticent in Moscow that I assumed his surname was Stainton. Meeting him again in London, he looked surprised when I asked him if I could call him Forrest – 'Mr Stainton sounds too formal' – and totally bemused as I continued, 'Forrest is a most unusual name.'
'Yes, it is my father's.'
Of course it is: his name is Stainton Forrest.

Of all the people I have spoken to, Stainton gave me the most heartfelt insight into Gilbert & George, one that I could not have gained from anyone else with the possible exception of Tyrone Dawson, their assistant who held the fort in Fournier Street while the rest of us were in Moscow.
It was said by Madame Cornuel in the seventeenth century that 'No man is a hero to his valet', but I have always found this a foolish remark for it depends on both the man and the valet. I prefer Lord Byron's contradictory couplet:

In short he was a perfect cavaliero,
And to his valet seemed a hero.

Presumably Madame Cornuel suspected that a valet is disillusioned by such proximity, and that could be true in certain cases. Stainton is no twentieth-century valet, but he is their cleaner and he has no illusions concerning Gilbert & George.
He met them at a low point in his life, and they changed it.
Stainton Forrest came from Jamaica in 1969 when he was 24 in search of work, and he found it in a foundry, building site, raw metal mill, and Ford motors – 'Everything.'
In 1981, when he met Gilbert & George, his marriage had broken up and he worked as a handyman in the Whitechapel Gallery where they were having a show. 'They watch me – see how I operate – and ask me

to join them. I hesitate for I do not understand …' He gives a quick smile but does not elucidate. 'Gilbert said, "We are good people, you won't regret it" and gave me a card.'

This was the start of a rare relationship. A hard, reliable worker, outstanding in his job, Stainton works as a cleaner today for Gilbert & George, the d'Offay Gallery and the Bank of England.

Though taciturn in Moscow, which he disliked, Stainton seemed a different person in the East End, forthcoming, almost voluble.

'They are the two nicest people I ever met in the whole world,' he told me. 'The only two humans I ever met. It's hard to explain the feeling – the way they made me feel wanted. When I met them I was really down – apart from the help of God, they are the only two who help revive me. To me, more than a friend, more than a brother, no words to say how good they are.'

His sons Paul and Jason have appeared in their pictures, and Paul accompanied his father when Gilbert & George invited them to their exhibition at the Guggenheim Museum in New York in 1985. 'I'm telling you – the greatest time in my life. I ask myself this question, "Is this really me, being here with my son, Paul?" And he say, "Dad, if you did come back and tell me all this, I'd have to ask myself is that really true? But seeing is believing".'

Since then, Stainton has gone with Gilbert & George to their exhibitions in Madrid, Bordeaux, and now Moscow.

I asked him with such unnecessary tact that he failed to understand me, if he ever felt embarrassed at being thrown into high society, seated next to the wife of the gallery's owner or an art collector of untold wealth. I did not repeat the story of the hostess, a Rothschild in France, who told them 'Now who shall sit where – eeny, meeny, miny, mo, catch a … Oh, for God's sake!' – covered with confusion – 'Please sit wherever you like!'

'Prejudice?' said Stainton. 'I never confront that at all. Ever. I wish half the world was like them. Then it would be a perfect world. If you can bury all the troubles of the world in a hole as they could, everyone could be treated as equals.'

Few people are so tedious as saints, and Gilbert & George were in danger of sanctification until Stainton allowed them a crucial defect: 'They don't want things to be too perfect.'

'Have you ever known them lose their temper?'

'Do I ever see it!' he exclaimed. 'I do! And you wouldn't like to see it. When George really loses it, he really loses it. When he's calmed down, you wouldn't believe it was him.'

'What causes it? Usually it's something quite trivial?'

'They are straightforward. They don't like anyone to come to them with crookedness. If you try to give them *less*, they don't like it. Their policy is good, but they're really upset if someone tries to put them down.'

I am sure this is correct. Once you gain their trust they respond unreservedly and forgive anything except betrayal. They have startled me with their insistence that people should be allowed to do whatever they want without criticism. When I protested that one person was cruel to strangers and another refused to work, Gilbert exclaimed, 'But that is all right! That is how they are!'

They are virulent about their critics – especially art critics – but their hostility is honest and open in refreshing contrast to the usual speciousness in the art world. Their loyalty is restricted; you cannot be loyal to a crowd.

Gilbert & George make their own rules, and unreserved tolerance towards their friends is one of them. The case of the poet and artist David Robilliard is revelatory: 'They push him, push him,' Stainton told me, 'and get him off the crowd. Gilbert and George helped him – so sad the moment he was uplifted was the moment he was cut off.'

They alone were by his bedside when he died of AIDS in the Middlesex Hospital. Championed by Gilbert & George he is now a minor cult in New York where an exhibition of his work in 1990 was accompanied by this statement from his two friends:

OUR DAVID

David Robilliard was the sweetest, kindest, most infuriating, artistic, foul-mouthed, wittiest, sexiest, charming, handsomest, thoughtful, unhappy, loving and friendly person we ever met. Over the nine years of our friendship David came closer to us than any other person. He will live forever in our hearts and minds.

Starting with pockets filled with disorganised writings and sketches he went on to produce highly original poetry, drawings and paintings. His truthfulness, sadness, desperation and love of people gave his work a brilliance and beauty that stands out a mile.

Gilbert & George 7 July 1990

Anyone who is fortunate to receive such friendship would strive to sustain it. This is another accomplishment; Gilbert & George bring out the best in their friends.

I asked Stainton if he was hurt by the labels people stick on them.

'As far as I'm concerned, every man has a life to live. For nine years I haven't seen anything like that. [He did not specify what 'that' might be.] People should get to know them before they talk.' As for the glibly applied label of 'fascist': 'They don't know what they're talking about. Some people even say they should move from Spitalfields.'

'Why?'

'I don't know. I love it so much. Oh my God!' he declared with startling passion for such an impassive man, 'when you mention Fournier Street I wake up. That's *the* house!' No wonder it glistens so contentedly.

As for criticism of the pictures: 'I wish people who disagree with their work could see them as they really are – two perfect men. People in the past try to fuck them up, if the papers had their way they would have Gilbert & George to close down, but there's no stopping them now. I feel so happy for them.'

'They are so generous. Do they use their money wisely?'

'Fellow artists criticise them. They made a book which should sell for £20 but they help it to sell for £12. At the AIDS show people said "fools – idiots – no person should give away so much money".'

The point is that they give it away to help others – including Stainton. 'They change my life completely. Meeting them makes life worth living. Being with them, walking with them, I feel like I've achieved something in life – a great feeling. I know I'll never, ever meet people like them again.'

Too good to be true? Not if you heard the conviction in Stainton's voice as he told me, 'If anything happened to either of them, I would take out my eyes and give to them.'

CHAPTER EIGHT

ARRIVAL OF THE MOTLEY COLLECTORS – AND ANTHONY D'OFFAY – AND DOLLY

Midweek in Moscow with Judy rushing to the airport to greet the VIPs who were flying in from various parts of the world to attend the exhibition. Altogether 34 people came to Moscow, including collectors who had lent their work – none had refused. I had a few incomprehensible words with Massimo Martino, reputedly the owner of fifteen Gilbert & Georges, while others remain strange, exotic names and I have little idea who they were or whether I met them: Isy Brachot; Ascan Crone; Desire Feuerle; Mr and Mrs Uwe Kraus and Wim Beeren, unlikely names which might have sprung from a novel about the *Titanic.*

Jean-Louis Froment, and Illeana Sonnabend, who runs a New York gallery which deals in Gilbert & George, were unable to continue to Moscow due to an air strike in Paris. Others in Moscow included Massimo and Francesca Valsechi, and Howard Reed from the Miller Gallery in New York.

Mirjana Winterbottom from the d'Offay flew in with the sole objective of finding a good restaurant where everyone could celebrate the following night.

David Goodwin from the Tate Gallery had flown in with James and Judy to ensure the safety of the quadruplet – *Death, Life, Hope, Fear* – and flew back to London after making sure that it was properly installed. I still find it mind-boggling that the Tate should send someone specifically to check on one of their purchases, and admirable.

Rudi Fuchs of the Gemeentemuseum in the Hague was especially welcome as one of Gilbert & George's closest friends and supporters. So was Wolf Jahn, their biographer, 'autor' of *Die Kunst Von Gilbert & George*, a weighty tome published by Thames and Hudson as *The World of Gilbert & George.*

ARRIVAL OF THE MOTLEY COLLECTORS

The least conspicuous were the most important: Anne and Anthony d'Offay who flew in on the Wednesday. This was my first encounter with the formidable man whose gallery bears his name. He is one of those men who are irresistible to women, and other men cannot understand why. With the aphrodisiac of success, he is sought after. The *New Statesman* ran a profile that same week which described him as 'a man whose business takes him to New York one week out of four, and who travels to Europe four or five times in the same period. This is someone who could say – without any recognition that most of us don't live like this – that he may see his friends and clients from Cleveland, Ohio, more frequently than those from South Kensington'. Gordon Burn made the brutal comment in the *Sunday Times Magazine* (30 September 1990) that his manner suggests 'both flaccidness and blind ambition, both the chapel of rest and the private vault'.

Anthony d'Offay's ambition is undeniable, but only the English would object to that. Not once did he impose his authority in Moscow; instead he seemed to prefer his anonymity. He is calculated to the point of ruthlessness, yet abstemious, and his charm is meticulous. He takes the trouble to do his homework beforehand and when he pays a compliment he aims it like a dart. Warned about this beforehand, I smiled outwardly and chuckled inwardly when he paid a tribute to my shirt as if it had been designed by Bakst. I have forgotten the exact words but they were fulsome. I have no recollection of the shirt, except it wasn't *that* good.

Anthony d'Offay, his wife and his gallery were hospitable throughout. He gave me his time one Saturday morning after our return to London. As we went upstairs to his offices in Dering Street he discovered he had the wrong keys and I seized the opportunity to suggest that we sat outside the pub next door which had tables and chairs. After all, it was opening time and a perfect warm September day. I detected a certain reluctance as he agreed, asking the barman for a mineral water, settling for a tonic, with a pained smile, when informed that the mineral water had run out.

'Ice and lemon?' said the barman jauntily.

'Certainly not,' Mr d'Offay replied fastidiously. I was tempted to add, 'And no plastic swords either.' Later, he was kind enough to ask me to lunch at a nearby fish restaurant even though he was fasting, which was somehow off-putting, and I regret that this proved impossible for I suspect he is excellent company when the notebooks are put aside.

As it was, he had made a rare concession. 'You don't mean you persuaded Anthony into that pub!' a former employee exclaimed. 'He hates pubs so much that we were forbidden to use it in case one of his clients saw us there and disapproved!'

In Moscow Anthony d'Offay seemed happy to be treated like the rest of us; in London I realised that he is far more equal than others.

'Am I right in saying that d'Offay is one of the top three or four galleries in London?'

He stared at me, disbelieving such naivety. 'I should hope so,' he remarked. 'We are the *only* large gallery dealing in contemporary art.'

I mumbled something about the Marlborough, referring to the new Glasgow Boys, Stephen Campbell and Stephen Conroy: 'Ten years from now, everyone will have forgotten them.'

'You think so?'

'I know so.'

'Is it true,' I persevered, 'that your annual turnover is £17 million?'

'Where did you get that figure?' he demanded.

'Less?'

'More. Twenty million would be closer.'

Phew! I thought, knocking back my gin while he took a dainty sip of his tonic and gave me a serpentine smile. I was beginning to sense that in no respect should Anthony d'Offay be underestimated.

His formidable reputation in the international art market has been invaluable to Gilbert & George, though their relationship has been of mutual advantage. Each, at times, has proved necessary to the other. They have known each other since the start of their careers and d'Offay had the wit to recognise their potential before the other dealers. Since then, he has given support without interference. There is a personal involvement too: at the opening of the new Hayward Gallery in 1972, George told d'Offay, 'Why don't you give Anne Seymour a kiss on behalf of all the artists?'

Today, Anne Seymour is Mrs d'Offay and her knowledge of contemporary art, acquired during her time as a curator of modern art at the Tate Gallery, enhances his.

Anthony d'Offay encountered Gilbert & George when he was a young man and saw their *Red Sculpture*. 'This totally changed the way I looked at something. I liked the tension between them; I liked their endearing quality of innocence on the one hand and knowingness on the other.'

I suggested that art critics were provoked unnecessarily by the puerile titles attached to some of the pictures. Had he ever tried to dissuade them?

'Oh no! It's very important that they deal with subjects that haven't already been burnt into the realm of art today. The fascist label? They're nice working-class boys who care for the people,' he stated impassively. 'If Gilbert & George were completely accepted, then they'd have cause to worry. Is any radical art completely accepted in its time? Beuys was not accepted in Germany, Warhol not in America. There is an interesting comparison between Warhol, Beuys and Gilbert & George who have turned their lives into works of art. Those are the three artists who attract very young people.'

'Would the young be equally attracted to Monet's water lilies?'

'We no longer accept that there's anything challenging about the water lilies. No longer a difficult question as it was in 1915.'

'Can you see the day when Gilbert & George receive their knight-hoods?'

'Absolutely.'

D'Offay's shrewd commercial instinct did not prevent his altruism in joining Gilbert & George by giving the profits from their show in 1989 to AIDS research, a remarkable gesture by a gallery and not properly appreciated at the time. Equally, he gave his whole-hearted support to the Moscow exhibition from the outset. I asked why he was so enthusiastic – did he regard it as important?

'Oh yes!' emphatically. 'A vast resource of humanity, untapped for contemporary art. A great longing and need for art.' Considering that none of the pictures were for sale and no commercial element was involved – not in the immediate future, at least – his participation proved the importance of Moscow's potential role in the international art market.

Since then, the exhibition has boosted Gilbert & George's prices in New York. At the time, he was fully aware of the probable repercussions – 'We are incredibly lucky to be here,' he told me then.

How does he see their future?

'Very rosy, but they have to be careful and look after themselves.'

'Do you mean physically?'

'The late forties are different from the late twenties.'

'Would you advise them how to direct their work?'

'No. I like to leave everything open. I always see what they want.'

Today, as seldom before, the championship of the right art gallery is crucial if the artist wishes to contend in the international market. Marlborough's skilful promotion of Francis Bacon changed his life with the first retrospective at the Tate. D'Offay's dedication to Gilbert & George, culminating in Moscow, has given them vital prestige.

The Collectors showed remarkable loyalty in taking the trouble to fly to Moscow in order to attend the exhibition.

Dolly J. Fiterman of the Dolly J. Fiterman Gallery in Minneapolis, whose good humour enchanted me, especially when she was arrested in the bar of the Belgrade Two Hotel.　　　Photo. Daniel Farson.

My favourite was Dolly J. Fiterman who came on her own from Minneapolis. I fell in love with her name as soon as I heard it, introducing her in the mordant tones of Walter Matthau – 'May I present Dolly J. Fiterman, President of the Dolly J. Fiterman Gallery Inc in Minneapolis.' She rose to the occasion beautifully.

Dolly is the perfect name for a lady who personifies American ebullience. Her energy made the rest of us look like limp lettuce. There could be those who consider her a figure of fun – if they have not met her. She *is* fun, which is something different altogether. She walks with the swing of a dancer and I was not surprised to read in a press cutting that she turned cartwheels all the way to the store in the small northern Minnesota town where she was born – 'She was a sheer ball of energy' her sister recalled. 'She could move heaven or earth for whatever she wanted.' Predictably, Dolly was a drum majorette at Mahnomen High School; less predictable she was Minnesota's first 'wild rice queen'.

The description of Dolly in the same cutting as 'Art dealer, collector and philanthropist' is too forbidding. With the eagerness of a child returning from a holiday abroad, she showed me a sheaf of snaps of her home with the health spa off the master bedroom, complete with Turkish and Finnish sauna and jacuzzi, and the 54-foot lap pool suspended from the second storey beneath a glass ceiling where she swims under the stars. These were interspersed with snaps of her family and confidential asides – 'The moment my daughter went on a diet she realised she was pregnant.'

The Dolly Fiterman Gallery was being transferred to the 'historic' Pillsbury Library at 100 University Avenue Southeast in Minneapolis, described as 'an architectural jewel built in 1904 in the *Beaux Arts*-style an impressive, miniature Versailles'.

Dolly! I could see her descending those stairs. Irrepressible Dolly! She is one of those fortunate people who forge an instant rapport, the antithesis to the sleek saluki American success story who rants at the slightest delay and travels with an entourage of secretaries and hairdressers. Dolly had the guts to fly in alone, which roused my instant curiosity. Why had she bothered? Judy told me that the collectors 'may not yet be sure what is happening but they know they want to be here', and this was confirmed by Dolly.

'I have two masterpieces by Gilbert & George and I just had to be here, and I've come here with love, so happy to be a part of it!'

The more I saw of Dolly the more I respected her, apart from possessing two qualities which I find irresistible: extreme innocence and immense wealth.

ARRIVAL OF THE MOTLEY COLLECTORS

Edward Fiterman was a Minneapolis financier and though Dolly is not Jewish herself, she inaugurated the Marc Chagall Memorial Forest in Israel on Edward's death in 1984, after 27 years of marriage, and pledged $1 million to Temple Israel for a new wing called the Dolly and Edward Fiterman Building. She has also contributed $250,000 to the Walker Art Centre's sculpture garden – sums which interested me strangely.

'Do you think, Mrs Fiterman,' I asked her after we announced our engagement that first evening in Moscow, 'that you will be able to keep me in a style to which I am unaccustomed?'

She laughed, nervously for once, for money is never a subject of mirth to those who have it. I noticed that Troy was taking an interest in her too, asking questions about the climate in Minneapolis, and so forth.

The virtue of Dolly is her taste in acquiring work by Picasso, Frank Stella, Andy Warhol, Milton Avery, Jim Dine, Robert Rauschenberg, Jasper Johns, the German Expressionists of the late 1980s, Andreas Schulze and Rainer Fetting, as well as Gilbert & George. 'My goal is to have a high-quality gallery on a par with the east coast, and give exposure to young talent.'

Mirjana Winterbottom had discovered the perfect restaurant, the Kolkhida, after her day's exploration, a rarity in Moscow with good Georgian food, an intimate atmosphere, and a charming old violinist who performed such party tricks as playing the violin on the top of his head. As we sat down, I noticed that Dolly, who had arrived earlier at the Ukraine, was missing, and Mirjana Winterbottom raced back to collect her. Dolly joined us and sat down beside me without a murmur of complaint at being forgotten. She had never met Gilbert & George although she possessed their two 'masterpieces', and said she was 'thrilled' when I asked if she would like me to introduce her. 'May I present Dolly J. Fiterman,' I said, and Gilbert & George rose with their usual courtesy and George's murmured chorus of 'Extraordinary ... how kind ... sweet'. She came back to me after several minutes, flushed with pleasure.

That was a good night in the Kolkhida, the best of our stay in Moscow, with the exuberance that everyone hoped to find in Russia. The small room was crowded, with three Armenian couples at a corner table where the men, like grizzly bears, fluctuated between tears and fisticuffs. The violin wailed, the vodka flowed – though the waiters tried to persuade us to drink Caucasian wine which was more expensive – and the evening ended as if in a scene from *Ninotchka* with the animated Russians bobbing up and down from their chairs as they declared a stream of toasts which gave them the excuse for knocking back the vodkas in a single gulp. Rudi Fuchs danced on a tiny table. The climax was reached when Gilbert followed him with a pirouette worthy of Chaplin. Usually a cautious drinker, I heard him exclaim earlier, 'Christ, this is crazy!' as someone poured him a lethal cognac. By now he was drinking like the rest of us.

The dinner came to an end but the night was too vigorous to run down and I went ahead with Dolly to the bar in the Belgrade Two Hotel. For some inexplicable reason, a Russian had presented me with a bouquet of flowers which I handed to Dolly with a suitable flourish, and she entered the hotel with her head held high carrying the flowers and her bottle of mineral water in the other hand. Five feet eight inches high, in her mid-sixties and dressed to kill, she looked terrific and was promptly arrested by a glum Russian soldier at the door who mistook her for a high-class Muscovite hooker.

'You know, Daniel,' she said after I talked her in, 'this is one of the *nicest* evenings I've had in all my life.'

Jill Ritblat, another popular arrival and a well-known collector, was interested in seeing Gilbert & George in a different context.

'On closer acquaintance would they turn out to be the prejudiced, racist, sexist, truculent drunks of repute, or would I retrieve the inscrutable courteous hosts that I had found in Fournier Street, or the affable guests they had been in my own house?' she wrote to me afterwards.

Charisma and star quality need a study of their own, but nothing breeds success like success. There's no doubt about the success of that famous image, twenty-odd years of it: the double act, the two iconic presences immaculately coiffed, shaved and shod, the unlikely attire (the old school sent up?), the ever arranged features.

Carefully timed entrances and exits are crucial to the image, as on our first evening when they arrived late for dinner accompanied by other principal players. Expectation had been mounting. Rumour had it they were exhausted, frustrated – the difficulties of hanging had been great – Russian lighting had been inadequate. How would it show? But no – their entrance was perfectly timed and they were exquisite – smiling, affable, polite to the unknowns, affectionate to the intimates. George poured vodka and gossiped, committed and expansive. My God, they were human after all.

Keith Davey was a late arrival. I noticed that Gilbert & George surround themselves with people who excel: not only exceptionally nice but also the best in their field. Stainton Forrest is more than a cleaner, their assistant, Tyrone Dawson, is so efficient that it is a pleasure to deal with

Rudi Fuchs and Anthony d'Offay attach the correct labels beside the pictures on opening day.

Photo. Daniel Farson.

him at a time when most people seem incapable of giving a straight answer. Raymond O'Daly is the best at hanging an exhibition; Keith Davey the best at recording it.

In Keith Davey's line of work, a snap or artistic impression is not good enough. It requires particular skill to reproduce a painting accurately. He told me that on one occasion Gilbert & George were dissatisfied with the colour reproduction of their latest pictures, and instead of letting this pass they objected to it firmly pointing out exactly what was wrong. Keith Davey recognised that they were in the right, scrapped the whole batch, and started the mammoth undertaking again, as pleased as they were when it proved successful.

When he records an entire exhibition, as he has done on several occasions for Gilbert & George, he is faced with a challenge that only a few photographers could overcome.

'Photographing these works does present a few problems,' he admits. 'When they started to produce the very large works such as *Drunk with God* and *Waking* I had to find a large enough wall to photograph them on. Judy Adam had a brainwave – what needs a very large space? The answer was an aeroplane and she came to an arrangement with the Hendon Air Museum which allowed us in after hours to use one of the hangar walls. I went there beforehand to select a suitable space, but the only wall large enough meant we had to place the camera underneath a Vulcan bomber to get far enough back. As there was a Sopwith Pup – a very small bi-plane – that looked as if it might cast a shadow from our lights, I asked if this could be moved and the director picked up the tail and wheeled it around: that is how you move it. That night in the museum I needed to shift the plane and a security guard who was watching us on his video monitor descended on us like a screaming sergeant major – a difficult moment to explain. It's never dull photographing Gilbert & George's work.'

CHAPTER NINE

BEGINNING TO UNDERSTAND MOSCOW

There is a curious musty smell to Moscow, hard to define and not so overpowering that it sets the nose atwitching, but it lurks. I suspect it comes from the fumes of inferior petrol which hang heavily in the airlessness.

In spite of the broad streets and views across the river to the seven tall Stalinist-baroque buildings like the Hotel Ukraine, I found the city claustrophobic and longed for rain. Gilbert described it as 'grey' and this is the colour, rather like rain itself, that lingers in the mind, providing a perfect contrast to the vivid dyes of Gilbert & George's work. I remember the sadness too: the reluctance of Russians to meet in hotel bars or restaurants, which made them nervous, preferring the intimacy of their one- or two-roomed apartments where we endured the stupefying boredom of waiting interminably in a well-decorated though crowded room with every inch of space turned to advantage, force-fed with cake especially prepared for the occasion so it would have been churlish to refuse, while the child watched Western cartoon videos on the television set interminably, a status symbol rarely switched off.

The views usually overlooked identical, shabby apartment blocks with a sort of playground below where the grass had long been trampled into lifelessness, and a number of spindly birch trees rising wretchedly as if they too were gasping for air. I should add that I have been to tower blocks in London which were more depressing, scarred with understandably fierce graffiti, but these in Moscow were among the best available.

A dismal and defeated city, rather than angry, the Muscovites had much to be angry about with the inevitable queues and the Western imposition of McDonald's.

When I entered my local Safeways after my return, I felt that a Russian housewife would break down and cry in the face of such abundance and would be bewildered by the choice. Conversely I was shocked by the *beriozka* shops in the big hotels where luxuries can be bought for hard currency which puts them beyond the reach of the Russians unless they deal in the black market as so many of them do. Perhaps they are angrier than I realised, for Bridget Kendall who works in Moscow for the BBC, notices, 'A new phenomenon – a resentment of foreigners and envy of what they have. Glasnost has allowed people to see what they are missing, and they feel angry that they have been deprived of so much!' She added that the standard of living is worse than when she was there as a student in the Seventies.

I did not experience this anger due to the friendliness of the Russian artists, though when I exclaimed over dinner on our first evening that the red caviar and smoked sturgeon was a wonderful treat, Sergei Klokhov's father beside me remarked with a bitter smile, 'It certainly is – *for us*!'

If I was a Russian I would be enraged by those hotel restaurants crowded with foreigners and Russians with hard currency or special permits. Endless humiliations for them, which made me feel humiliated too, though the Russians might consider this to be self-indulgent, even condescending.

Because there was no bar in the Hotel Ukraine, we tended to use the restaurant as our rendezvous, until it was closed for redecoration, when we had to wait interminably in that unlovely lobby. Most of us surfaced bleary-eyed at noon unless there was a special appointment, though not Gilbert & George who remained remarkably chipper. On one occasion, as I waited with James, a youngish man who looked as if he was made of teak lurched towards our table and demanded of James: 'Russian?'

'No, I'm not,' said James, politely and calmly, while I held my breath.

'You are Russian?' the man demanded.

'No.'

For a moment I thought the man was going to strike James in the face, and this was certainly in the balance, but he moved on. A few minutes later he was escorted out. Obviously he had been drinking and this had aggravated a deep, inner resentment, provoked by the sight of so many people feeding their faces in a setting where he was excluded. This was disturbing because one could sympathise with his rage. I always found it disconcerting to eat in such a privileged fashion, denied to the Russians themselves unless they were privileged. Seldom have I encountered such class-consciousness.

A salesman of masks of former Soviet leaders. I bought 'Stalin' while the man, a born comic, put on a Brezhnev mask and delighted the crowd in Izmailovsky Park with his lugubrious impression of the aged political dinosaur.   Photo. Daniel Farson.

(From left to right) Julian Cole, who was making a film on Gilbert & George and appears in their picture, SEE (1987); James, Judy, and Gilbert & George in Red Square with the familiar cupolas of St Basil's beyond.

Photo. Daniel Farson.

I love walking through foreign cities: this is one of the pleasures of life – Paris, with the zest of discovering St Germain; Venice, though that first ecstatic view is unsurpassed. I did not feel this in Moscow. People talk of the beauty of the city, and I might have had my eyes opened if

BEGINNING TO UNDERSTAND MOSCOW

Christopher Hope had been my guide. As it was, I used his book, *Moscow, Moscow!*, but the cathedral which he recommended at the corner of the Kremlin was inadmissible, and I was not allowed to enter St Basil's.

The richness of these cathedrals is evident and I savoured the odd detail, but Moscow as a whole did not tempt me as a place to wander. The vistas of the Kremlin and the Red Square are momentous, but even these have a picture-postcard remoteness and I never felt I was a participant as I do in Istanbul with my morning walk from Pera across Galata Bridge with the street vendors and men fishing and that extraordinary skyline beyond of mosques and minarets which never disappoints, although Richard Hannay dismissed them in *Greenmantle* as mere 'factory chimneys'. The bridge across the Moscva river held no such thrill; simply a place to cross from one side to the other. I have said that I felt I belonged when I arrived in Russia, but I felt a stranger too.

Of course there were bonuses: the splendid frontage of the Bolshoi Theatre; the brides and grooms laying their flowers beside the Eternal Flame under the walls of the Kremlin; a Saturday-morning drive with Troy in his baseball cap and latest trainers to Ishmail, or Izmailova Park, with the carefree atmosphere so lacking in the centre of the city. Sizzling barbecues, smoking bonfires, a jazz band, and proof of the new freedom as smiling young men sold Gorby dolls with the smaller figures inside of Brezhnev and Krushchev, until a tiny Stalin disclosed a tinier Lenin. This cost me £20 in hard currency, well worth it as I saw the disappointment when I handed the wrapped doll to a friend in London saying 'I've bought you a Russian doll, you know, with the smaller dolls inside', only to be rewarded by her cries of delight as Gorby, instead of the usual *matryoshka*, was revealed. I also bought a mask of Stalin from a middle-aged man who was evidently a born actor as he put on a Brezhnev mask and delighted the crowd as he harangued them with the familiar wagging finger and spoke the lugubrious, discredited platitudes. As I walked back, the young man who sold me the Gorby doll gave me a simple wooden toy of a bear sawing a log with a man, which one can slide backwards and forwards. 'Gorby' was scribbled on the bear; Litva on the saw; Sayoopis on the man. Of little value but a cheerful dissenting souvenir which stands in silhouette on the window in front of me as I write this now.

I went on my own to the Pushkin Museum for James was busy and Gilbert & George declined with one of their infuriating proclamations – 'Art is for art students, not artists,' said Gilbert; 'We have come to be looked at, not look,' said George.

BEGINNING TO UNDERSTAND MOSCOW

The *entire* museum proved glorious, with the great collection of the Impressionists as the climax. Richard Salmon told me later that he had been overwhelmed by the Vuillard, the finest he had seen.

Walking back was wearisome in the Moscow heat and an overcast sky with the promise of rain unfulfilled. Stalin's gigantic motorways seemed threatening in their impersonality, with no chance of a taxi until a friendly family took pity on me and drove me back to the Hotel Ukraine, reward by Marlboro.

Though Moscow had an oppressive sense of doom, it was invigorated like a city in the last days of siege as my father had found it in 1914. Sad, oppressive, yet enthralling.

I loved Russia because of the volatile Russians, with the marked exception of the Soviet women in positions of authority who show a sadistic satisfaction in their unhelpfulness, with a terse '*Niet!*'

I even grew fond of the Ukraine, as I imagine prisoners must do – 'Mine is a better Nick than yours' – though I envied the Heineken Bar in the National. Scribbling my notes in a corner one afternoon, after walking through the park below the Kremlin walls, I witnessed a startling scene: a group of young Englishmen who were hard to identify, being too untidy to be army yet not sufficiently brutish to be footballers, though they embarked on a series of songs that might have shamed a rugby team. The prostitutes at the next table had abandoned hopes of me and watched goggle-eyed, trying to look decently shocked while still available. A climax was reached as two of the Englishmen performed their version of *Old Macdonald Had a Farm* simulating every sexual act known to man and beast, finally dropping their trousers and exposing themselves, an exhibition which disconcerted the prostitutes, who might have been invisible as far as the Brits were concerned, and who were no longer certain how they should react. What fascinated me was the delicacy of the singers' movements with a precision gained from long practice or careful rehearsal, executed with the effeminancy of a minuet. The effect was rather beautiful in spite of the obscenity, yet completely unEnglish, more like an Indian troupe entertaining the Fringe at an Edinburgh Festival.

For a moment I was tempted to move to a nearer table in an attempt to eavesdrop and find out who they were and why they were celebrating. When I decided it was time to leave this unusual bar where the entertainment had not raised an eyebrow apart from mine and those of the prostitutes, I coincided with the Brits. Suddenly their exuberance had been deflated and they looked decidedly glum in the street outside the National.

BEGINNING TO UNDERSTAND MOSCOW

'On holiday?' I asked one of them, a leading question which received the contempt that it deserved.

'Holiday? Here? You'd have to be out of your bloody mind to come *here* for a holiday!'

'Sport?' I persisted.

'*Telecom.*'

I left it at that.

Prostitutes are abundant in Moscow, tolerated by the hotels for the sake of hard currency and the hand-outs to the staff, and also by the KGB who believed, naively, that they might gain useful information from their Western clients. They varied from young and attractive in the Heineken Bar that afternoon, to considerably tougher in the Belgrade Two that night where one burly lady decided that I was target for the night and bit me on the cheek. George found this hilarious; I was less amused – 'I hate to think where her teeth have been, and to make it worse she looks like *me*!' She proved persistent, furious that I rejected her.

These bars were tacky with little attempt at decoration or friendly service, ingrained by years of passive acceptance. What made them so interesting, apart from the flattering gauntlet of the tarts, were the other visitors from abroad, with the bond of stranded passengers: a smiling Mexican who listened so intelligently that I failed to notice he did not understand a word we said; an androgynous Finn who wanted to learn everything about Oscar Wilde; a pleasant English TV producer research-ing a programme for *This Week* on the new political party which resembles our National Front in its anti-semitism: 'What an odd lot you are!' he said of us. And this was true: Gilbert & George in their identical tweed suits and floral ties; James Birch entirely dressed in black; Troy, Stainton and Judy, apparently innocence personified; and myself – like survivors of a wreckage thrown together.

Consequently we had the opportunity to know each other to an extent that would have been impossible in normal circumstances, just as strangers abroad reveal the most intimate details about their private lives with the assumption that they will never meet again.

Other evenings were spent in Russian homes. Sergei Klokhov, at the top of his mysterious tree, lives in one of the grander back streets with echoes of former splendour, in an apartment which he calls his studio with high ceilings and fine carpets brought from the Soviet Republics and silver from Kazakhstan. Waited on like a Turkish pasha by two attractive Russian women (it seems that Russian men in any position of authority not only keep one mistress but often two) we were served an endive salad, a rare luxury, followed by a distraught carcass of lamb. I mentioned the Ukrainian demonstration I had seen that afternoon beside the looming statue of one of their greatest poets, and Sergei growled like the bear that he resembles: 'If they wish to be nationalistic, then the Russians will become nationalistic too.'

In my ignorance, though I suspect it was shared by many, I thought of Russia as indivisible, disregarding the obvious fact that the USSR meant exactly that – a Union of Soviet Republics. Sergei Klokhov put me straight with his anger against the Republican movements, startling us with his explosive declaration that if they continued Russia would retaliate even if it meant bloodshed and a form of civil war. The very idea that there could be *Russian* sovereignty as against Ukranian was new to me and helped to explain the subsequent appeal of Boris Yeltsin, even though his form of nationalism for the Russians is economic rather than military. Once understood, his appeal became obvious: why support the Republicans and go short ourselves, especially as we – the Russians – receive no thanks but increasing resentment?

I am sure that if I were a Muscovite, I should feel equally exasperated by Georgian demands for independence, especially in the knowledge that people in Tblisi have food in their shops and few queues outside them.

Sergei Klokhov remains the most formidable and puzzling man I met in Soviet Russia. Like many powerful men he had moments of cosiness and I had no compunction in teasing him or arguing against his more outrageous assertions, and he did not seem to mind. At the same time, I doubt if it would turn a hair in his tousled beard to have me killed, a supposition reinforced by the tortures he would have inflicted on James if some money had not been repaid. These were described in such sadistic detail and with such relish that none of us laughed. When he placed a live scorpion on Judy's knee, brought by the manager of his snake farm, a man burnt by the sun, his face scarred by cobra-bites, and literally paralytic from vodka, it occurred to me that Klokhov was sinister. Conversely, he could be *charming*. Like Moscow, he was a man of contrasts – with him the blazing sun or darkest shadows.

On a lighter note, Sergei entertained us with the outline of a film he hopes to produce on the famous statue by Vera Mouchina of the worker and the peasant girl brandishing a hammer and sickle, the Soviet symbol chosen in an artistic competition in 1922.

This glistening, gigantic, metallic, though hollow, statue, has become symbolic for me as well. I photographed Gilbert & George beside it as one of the many locations which they endured with infinite patience.

BEGINNING TO UNDERSTAND MOSCOW

Sergei recounted the story behind the statue's erection at the historic Paris exhibition in 1925 which mingled triumph and tragedy. First it had to be approved by Stalin, then dismantled for the daunting journey across Europe by train into sections which were low enough to pass under the numerous bridges. Once it reached Paris, in a race against time, the Soviet workmen put it together again with the help of French girls who gave it a final polish. Intoxicated by the freedom of the West, not to mention French wine and Russian vodka, the jovial Russians became as great an attraction as the statue itself and news of their affairs with the French girls permeated back to Moscow. Shocked by such decadence, Stalin ordered their immediate return to Moscow and, no doubt, to points further east. They were not heard of again.

After we left Sergei's, we had an 'early night'. Returning to the Ukraine shortly before one, we decided against another bedroom party and James asked me if I had a sleeping pill. After I delivered it, I padded back down the corridors and heard the phone ringing in my bedroom. I put down my cases, struggled with the lock, and hurried inside in case this was an urgent summons from the *Sunday Telegraph* who were due to publish my piece on Gilbert & George that Sunday. By English time, it was ten o'clock. Instead it was just a hooker asking for cigarettes, and after reading for a few minutes I turned out the light and slept soundly. I needed to. The Moscow marathon was so punishing that my stamina still surprises me. Even James, so much younger and fitter, recorded 'Feel terrible' as the usual start to his daily notes. I felt rested and virtuous after my early night until I noticed something – or, rather, the absence of something – and felt the chill of panic. My camera case had vanished. I was certain I had brought it back from Sergei's with my larger canvas bag containing books, and wondered, for a moment, if a thief had entered the room during the night. As this was improbable, I assumed it must be concealed behind the chair – fallen under the bed – below the curtain – until there was nowhere else to look. Then I remembered that ringing telephone and my haste as I unlocked the door, putting down my cases as I did so. Of course! In my anxiety I raced inside carrying one of the bags, meaning to retrieve the other the moment the call was finished, but the door closed behind me and I forgot.

My camera case had lain outside all night. Could it be there now? I did not suspect a Russian, but I did have fears about another foreign visitor.

I opened the door to find an empty corridor; even so, it might have been handed in to the floor lady at her desk near the lifts where she gave us our keys, and I hurried down the corridor in my bare feet which

Part of the fun of Moscow was the return to schooldays with midnight 'dorm' feasts in James's bedroom, because he had most of the tuck and booze brought from England. Russian artists and officials usually joined us, though this shows me (from left to right) with George, Julian Cole and Troy.

created such astonishment that the floor lady called to her friends as if they had never seen such things before.

'Forget my feet,' I said testily. 'Have you seen my camera case?' I mimed the loss of it to little effect though she pointed to an office a few doors away where a grander supervisor sat behind a desk, polishing her nails. 'Niet,' she replied simply when I explained my loss. Decidedly niet.

Back in my bedroom, I sat down and took stock. It could hardly have been worse. Not only were my two cameras in that case, including my ancient and much-loved Rolliflex, but also documents and money. Without them, there was little point in continuing to the Caucasus. I telephoned Judy Adam in her bedroom, but this was just a squeal for help.

Suddenly a knock on the door, and there was the largest, ugliest woman I had seen in Moscow, though her face was partly concealed by

A common occurence nowadays, a demonstration of Ukrainians demanding their freedom took place one evening, near the Hotel Ukraine and a massive statue of their leading poet. With a priest in vestments, candles and chanting, it was well-conducted, almost subdued, though the anguish could be seen on their faces.   Photo. Daniel Farson.

her bifocals. She shoved the camera case towards me which seemed to leap into my arms like a long-lost dog, and as I embraced this suddenly beautiful cleaning-woman, she explained with gestures that she had found the case outside the door and had looked after it. I hurried to the drawer where I kept my cigarettes and gave her two packets of Marlboro, thanking her profusely, and she left the room beaming. Yet she had restored my livelihood – two packets of cigarettes as her reward – how could I be so mean? Padding down the corridor again, I found her cubby-hole and pressed two £5 notes into her hand.

As I related this to Gilbert & George and Judy in the makeshift dining-room downstairs, we were joined by James Birch who looked like Dracula at dawn.

'Are you sure that was a sleeping pill?' he asked, 'and not an upper?' I assured him it was, and he explained that he had taken half of it at first with little effect. The second half proved an equal failure: 'I lay there wide awake and heard this strange noise coming from the corner "Crunch; crunch; CRUNCH!" As my bedside light didn't work, I had to turn on my bathroom light and there was this large rat devouring the last of my chocolate biscuits.'

'Oh, come on,' said Judy, 'you had the DTs.'

James ignored this and continued, 'So I put on my socks and shoes and lay there clutching my crucifix.' This had been given to him by Misha's sister and nearly caused his arrest as he was stopped by a soldier on his way back to the hotel, who thought it was a pistol. Fortunately Misha was with him and explained it was a large crucifix.

'But why is it black?' asked the soldier.

'All right, we shall paint it white,' said Misha to reassure him. Now the iron crucifix had come into its own.

'You mean you were going to hold the crucifix up, to ward it off as if it were a vampire rat?' asked Judy.

'Don't be ridiculous. I was going to hit it.'

'Were you able to sleep?' I asked him.

'Not a wink.'

George had been listening intently, first to my account of the missing camera, then to James Birch about his rat.

'Serves you both right,' he declared unsympathetically. 'That will teach you not to have an early night.'

'George is right,' Gilbert agreed. 'You should never go to bed *half-drunk*. That can be *disastrous*!

CHAPTER TEN

THE RUSSIAN REACTION

In 1989, I contributed to a colloquium, 'The Church and the Visual Arts today: partnership or estrangement?', organised at Winchester Cathedral by Canon Keith Walker. I was appalled to see men of the church apparently nodding in agreement when a member of the staff of the Tate Gallery encouraged them to believe that Gilbert & George and Andy Warhol were among the greatest spiritual artists of our time. I had a vision of lurid stained-glass windows, with titles like *Marilyn* and *Dick Seed* rising up above the altars of parish churches and cathedrals throughout the land.

Peter Fuller, *Modern Painters*

The Russians found a spiritual content in Gilbert & George which eluded the English critics such as Peter Fuller.

Mikhail Mikheyev, the head of art promotion in the USSR's Union of Artists, worked closely with James Birch throughout and has stayed with him in England. He was the most important Russian to be actively involved with the exhibition, apart from Sergei Klokhov, who kept his distance from the others and worked independently.

Mikhail felt the project was too daring when it was first suggested by James, though the Muscovites had already seen such controversial artists from the West as Rauschenberg and Tinguely.

'After my meeting with Gilbert & George in London all my reservations disappeared. Transferring personal sympathies from a painter on to his creation is a dangerous path for a critic to follow, though it seems to me that the individual social stand of the artist is always reflected in that which he creates. Where Gilbert & George are concerned, one can even extend this notion further.

THE RUSSIAN REACTION

'They do not aspire to rise above the audience, to condescend or to withdraw. On the contrary, in every work they stress that they are no different from us – only they are more daring, more talented, have greater foresight and are more generous than us. This is why they are prepared to open up not only the doors of their castle [in Fournier Street] but also the doors to the most intimate corners of their souls.'

Mikhail Mikheyev makes no reference to the allegation that the USSR Union of Artists were promoting 'two homoerotic fascists'. Curiously, homosexuality does not *seem* to exist in Russia where it is illegal, though the late Tom Driberg and Robert Mackenzie tracked down an appropriate public lavatory with Geiger-counter speed. When it was suggested to the Marlborough Gallery that a couple of Francis Bacon's paintings might cause offence they were withdrawn, to the artist's annoyance, and Miss Beston asked, casually, if there were homosexuals in Moscow. 'Oh yes,' Klokhov told her airily, 'all in Lubiyanka!' The homosexuality of Tchaikovsky, and bisexuality of the film director Eisenstein, who cast his lover as the young Ivan the Terrible, is not discussed.

In the event, the abundance of young men in the paintings, which upsets the English critics, scarcely caused a frisson in Moscow. The Russians seemed uninterested in this aspect of their work. Meanwhile Gilbert & George forged a rapport that was remarkable to witness. As I wrote at the time for the *Sunday Telegraph* the Russians *loved* them, possibly mistaking them for English milords in their three-buttoned tweed suits.

'Gilbert & George have been touched by the warmth and generosity of the Russians who have done their utmost to please them. It is not too fanciful to claim that part of their immense popularity is due to their relevance. The cover of their catalogue is a picture called *One World* and this is deliberate as the catalogue copy shows: "A show like this has got to have a new vision," said George, "speaking for its time. More than anyone we believe in individuals, not parties or political movements. We have always been anti-communists."'

Their anti-communism gave their popularity in Moscow an added irony.

At one of the parties in James Birch's bedroom, where we grew emotional yet never tired, Anatoly Ryznikov, the head of the international relations department of the Union of Artists, and an exceptionally sympathetic man, spoke eloquently about the Russian affection for this unlikely duo: 'Russia is a special country. If someone meets you and loves you, it is for ever. First loves are the most important.'

THE RUSSIAN REACTION

The climax was a special luncheon held in their honour in the fine Union of Artists' building, attended by their president, Thair Salakov. In a country where protocol is still paramount, this was a singular endorsement. In a brief speech he told them, 'A few years ago, during the period of stagnation, you would not have been allowed to stage a show like this at all, but certainly not before the first of May. That's what makes it so marvellous.'

'How kind,' murmured George. 'Extraordinary!'

Afterwards, we wondered about the significance of the first of May. No one had the answer but everyone agreed that such an innovative exhibition was in tune with the new mood in Moscow.

The start to Opening Day had been inauspicious. The sleepless night had left James exhausted, appearing melancholy. I could see the impression this made on the Russians who found his stillness and his bedroom eyes infinitely romantic, unaware that his eyes looked as if they needed dusting because he yearned to be in his bedroom, alone and fast asleep. Without the rat.

Last-minute problems were being solved. These had proved surprisingly few. Gilbert & George had kept their patience throughout although they were visibly irritated when someone asked them to pose for photographs in the queue outside McDonald's, and another playing chess in Gorky Park. George was adamant: 'We would never pose outside McDonald's in London, and we don't play chess, so it wouldn't be true.'

Gilbert had been worried that the lighting was too dull, especially as the walls were beige instead of glistening white as intended for there had not been time for whitewash to dry after the unexpected exhibition of the Lenin commemorative stamps. By now the rooms had been brightened by spotlights and Gilbert was satisfied, though the extra light had caused a power cut in two areas, plunging them into darkness.

The pictures were in place. Raymond O'Daly and his Russian team were congratulated by Gilbert & George who recognised the effort involved, often beyond the call of duty as they worked throughout the night, but it occurred to me that this would be taken for granted by the Russians later, for people rarely understand the effort required in hanging an exhibition. Raymond O'Daly looked creased from lack of sleep though plainly pleased that he had beaten the deadline with several hours to spare. These were spent in cleaning up the debris, while Anthony d'Offay and Rudi Fuchs attached the labels beside the appropriate pictures.

THE RUSSIAN REACTION

The result was sensational: cascades of colour leaping from one room to another – the sheer immensity dazzling. On second thoughts, I decided that the Russians would not take the hanging for granted in this particular case. They might not understand *how* it was achieved, but they would find the impact overwhelming. Art should shock if only to delight, and this was the shock of exhilaration. The Tate picture in four parts covered an entire wall, the length of a small aircraft hangar. With no pantechnicon in the world – or Aeroflot capable of carrying pictures of such prodigious length, how was this possible? After this initial shock with the dawning realisation of the separate panels, there was the further shock of the subject matter.

'What will the Russians make of them?' I asked Marina, our interpreter. 'Will they be shocked?'

Anxious not to commit herself too far, she chose her words carefully. 'Not shock. Only interest in the freedom of expression and technique. Something quite new to our country. Later there may be other impressions: maybe compare them to mass culture – maybe "Why only men in the pictures?"' She shrugged as if she had gone too far. 'But technically *fantastic*.'

'How do you want the Russians to react?' I asked Gilbert, who was looking unusually animated, and laughed as he gave me the answer: 'I want them to say "What the fuck is that?" That would be the nicest compliment of all.'

I was glad to see Gilbert & George so happy, and thankful that I had come to terms with their work and was able to share in their excitement. By now I liked them so much that it would have been odious to pretend.

As I have mentioned, I felt from the outset that critics expect Gilbert & George to deliver a message which the artists have no interest in delivering, a common critical vice. The dislike is mutual, if derisive on their part: 'British art critics are racist because they are only interested in art which comes from wine-growing countries. The educated bigot in Britain just likes foreign art.'

'Everything circles around sex,' says Gilbert. 'The art world is narrow-minded and cannot accept what's completely honest.'

'The general public accept it quite easily,' says George. 'That's why we like flowers and plants – everything's fucking.'

Gilbert takes over in their conversational relay: 'Every young person who goes to an art gallery is looking for his freedom. I believe our art form is the most modern and will be the form of the future.'

When I mentioned the devastating comment by Peter Fuller that

The Moscow Exhibition, 1990.

Photo. Keith Davey.

The Moscow Exhibition, 1990.

Photo. Keith Davey.

The Moscow Exhibition, 1990.

Photo. Keith Davey.

Listening to the Exhibition opening speeches, Moscow 1990.

Photo. Keith Davey.

With the speeches over, the people flooded into the galleries to see the pictures. Moscow 1990.

Photo. Keith Davey.

Attendance remained high throughout the duration of the Exhibition.

The Poster

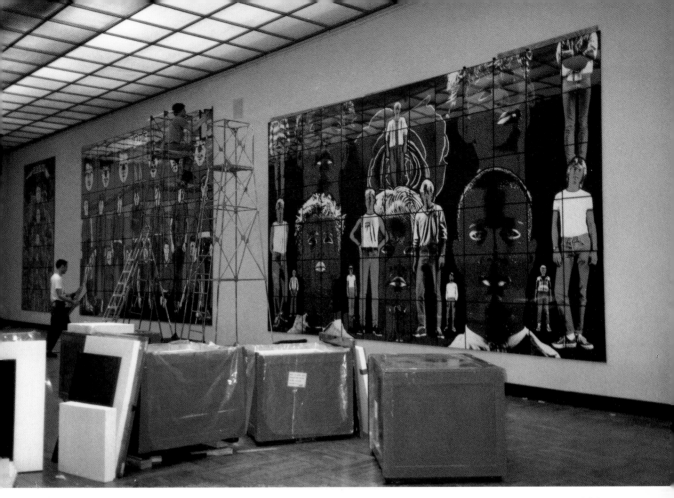

Because they are made up of panels – a thousand for the forty-four pictures displayed – these could be packed in chests and transported across Europe by lorry, and then reassembled. The effect of the massive works was stunning; one could see the Russians thinking, 'How is this possible?'

their work lacks feeling, it was one of the few times that I saw Gilbert annoyed. 'Our paintings are *filled* with feeling, that's why people either love it or hate it.'

'Our test,' added George, 'is to show a modern painting to the man in the street. If he's not sure, we feel it's wrong. It's not of its time. We offer difference, freedom. We hate conformity. We don't believe people need to be educated in Fine Art; the artist should speak directly to the viewer, not in terms of art history.'

Walking through another exhibition on the way to their own, Gilbert turned to me triumphantly as he pointed at the pictures by Russian artists which he found derivative. 'I don't think every artist would work here, like Auerbach or Kiefer. They have them already. Look over there – it's an Auerbach!'

Like two waxwork figures about to be unveiled, Gilbert & George wait for Keith Davey's group photograph while the rest of us mill around them, including Dolly Fiterman, Anthony d'Offay and Troy.

Photo. Daniel Farson.

George agreed. 'It's got to have a *new* vision, speaking for its time.'

While we toured the emptying rooms and Anthony d'Offay added the labels, James had gone directly to the kitchen staff – 'to the bottom rather than the top officials who would only delay things' – to arrange for the food for the Private View party, spending over two days in negotiation and paying 1,500 roubles to the staff with the inevitable gift of 200 cigarettes and four cans of lager to the cook and his assistant. With cigarettes subsequently rationed to 100 a month, it is easy to understand why this is the hardest currency of all.

Photo. Keith Davey.

Some of the friends, collectors, helpers and other V.I.P.'s photographed just before the exhibition opened.

1 Stainton Forrest, cleaner and companion to Gilbert and George   2 Richard Salmon, collector and London Gallery owner   3 Elena Bespalova, Russian art critic   4 Sergei Klokhov, James Birch's counterpart in Moscow, instrumental in arranging the exhibition   5 Mrs Armi Kraus 6 Bernd Barde, Printer   7 Uwe Kraus, Printer, Publisher and friend of the artists   8 Wolf Jahn, the author of 'The art of Gilbert and George'   9 Troy, Writer and Gilbert & George enthusiast   10 Dolly Fiterman, collector who flew in from Minneapolis   11 Paul Barratt, who acted as security guard for the pictures transported across Europe   12 James Birch, who initiated the exhibition in the first place   13 Rosemarie Barde   14 Anthony d'Offay of the Anthony d'Offay Gallery   15 Judy Adam, who co-ordinated the exhibition with James Birch   16 Rudi Fuchs, director of the Gemeentemuseum in the Hague   17 The Author, clutching his beloved Rolleiflex after it escaped   18 Anne d'Offay   19 Julian Cole, film-maker   20 Raymond O'Daly, who had the arduous task of hanging the pictures 21 + 22 Gilbert and George

THE RUSSIAN REACTION

With some difficulty we returned to the Hotel Ukraine to change, for it had started to snow and taxis swept by or were caught just before they reached us – exactly like London. Finally, Gilbert & George and I stopped a private car with the ubiquitous promise of Marlboro and we were driven back.

Strict instructions to return by three pm in time for Keith Davey's group photograph were jeopardised by lack of transport at the appointed time and the usual game of hide and seek in the lobby. I told Dolly I would look for Troy but by the time I found him she had disappeared and he invited me to his bedroom for a drink with Stainton instead. As time meandered past I started to panic and lost my temper as our taxi stopped at the wrong entrance to the Central House of the Artists and we traipsed interminably around finding no arrows or signs to the exhibition. Our invitation cards were studied with blank incomprehension, even though one side was printed in Russian. 'We've missed the photo,' I snapped at Troy, who was unperturbed, adding, 'and all for a bloody drink', which was not at all characteristic. We arrived to find that others were still on their way, though Dolly had made it on her own in the Zandra Rhodes dress she had mentioned to me earlier. 'I have a plain black ensemble,' she had explained, 'but also a Zandra Rhodes she made for me. It's not flashy, it's decorated with [it sounded like *snails*] but it's … well, striking!'

'The Zandra Rhodes,' I told her. 'After all, it *is* a celebration.'

I half dreaded and quarter hoped to see Dolly in one of Zandra's zanier outfits, so I was relieved to find her in a black-and-white, highly decorated dress that was striking yet surprisingly restrained. Her smile would have won the occasion, anyhow.

Conversely, Troy was upset that the special suit he hoped to wear for the Opening had not been flown out as arranged, though his checked jacket was first-class. James wore a tie; Stainton a white jacket; and Gilbert & George appeared as usual in their three-button suits.

The Press Conference followed at four. If you have seen the newsreels of the Nuremberg Trials you will understand why I found it so funny. James sat there dark in costume and grey in mood with Gilbert & George expressionless in the dock beside him, plainly guilty. Klokhov lurked at the far end of the table on the dias as if he wished to separate himself from the other Russians, as indeed he did, dressed down for the occasion in a peasant smock reminiscent of Rasputin. At the near end, the Russian lady interpreter was smart in frills and furbelows, though less so in the English language, having convinced her colleagues that she knew more than she did. More than 100 Soviet reporters were present.

THE RUSSIAN REACTION

'Are you going to make any speeches?' I asked Gilbert & George beforehand.

'Our speeches are on the walls,' replied George succinctly. James spoke on their behalf and told me afterwards 'I was so exhausted and shaken from tiredness that I felt none of the usual fear as I read my speech'. I noticed that he observed the protocol meticulously, thanking the Soviets who made the exhibition possible. In his turn, Mikhail Mikheyev was complimentary to James. Klokhov stayed silent. Then Gilbert & George answered questions.

Misha (Mikhail Mikheyev) describes the scene from the Soviet viewpoint: 'The artists, who are wearing their traditional suits, buttoned-up-to-the-top look, amongst this colourful crowd, more like two office workers who have accidentally wandered into the Private View. As I watched these two Performance experts, I could not but feel that this whole affair was itself a Performance.

'And this Performance began within the first few minutes of the Press Conference. Instead of the statutory provocative questions put to the artist, journalists politely expressed their interest in the means of execution of each piece and the reasons behind this choice of technique. I think that if in place of Gilbert & George there had been two bearded, bare-footed hippies in ripped jeans (the archetypal trendy artists) the Press Conference would have taken a very different turn. After it ended, the two artists confessed to having not expected such a loyal reception. I tried to explain this as Russian hospitality.'

I, too, was surprised by the concentration on the technique rather than the subject matter. To start with, the questions were predictable and though the answers were predictable too, I found that they added to my understanding of Gilbert & George, and wrote some of them down, starting with their belief that their art crosses all boundaries.

'We believe the camera is the modern brush.' (Gilbert)

'We believe in the picture looking at the viewer, not the viewer looking at the picture.' (Gilbert)

'Civilisation will not stop here.' (George)

'We want to be part of that change.' (Gilbert)

'We are making pictures like people always made pictures but we are using modern forms relevant to our time. We always work together – it's a partnership.' (jointly)

'Are you well known?' asked a Russian.

'Yes, of course,' George smiled at such absurdity, though this failed to rouse a titter from the reporters.

Inevitably the loaded question came at last. 'Is your work deca-dent?'

'What is decadence, you tell me?' Gilbert responded.

'We believe that art that only speaks to art is decadent,' said George. 'Art which only talks to specialists, art which is élite is deca-dent. Our art is appreciated by different people and nationalities, there-fore it is a kind of moral art.'

'We are not against being decadent ourselves!' Gilbert added with his inimitable humour which was both so carefree yet aimed so carefully.

The tension broke, and another reporter dared to ask why so many of the pictures were based on themselves.

'We are showing the world all our inner souls,' replied Gilbert. Someone else mentioned Blake: 'Blake was a kind of genius,' said George, 'but we're not interested in being influenced in that way.'

'You're not very social?' someone suggested, and for once Gilbert & George 'blew their cover': 'Just wait for two or three hours!' which raised a big laugh, especially from the Russians who already knew their high spirits.

Judy Adam closed the Conference by announcing that books on Gilbert & George by the German art historian Wolf Jahn were available. Surprisingly, a Russian reporter protested that it was 'more important to talk to the artists themselves.'

'Surely it is more important to see our *work*!' Gilbert corrected him with another disarming smile, and the Conference ended with laughter and applause as 'Gilbet and Jorjo', to use one of the Russian names for them – another verged, perilously, on 'Gilberta and Georgia' – went upstairs to the grand Opening.

Mikhail Mikheyev describes this as a triumph. 'Quite honestly I had not seen such a lively and intriguing opening at the Central House of Artists for quite some time.' Referring to the lavish catalogues, post-cards, badges and posters given to the guests he concluded, 'Such dedi-cated and thorough work could not have failed to bring results, and these were evident in every aspect of this marvellous exhibition.'

Even so, protocol reared its tedious head with a plenitude of speeches. The British Ambassador, Sir Roderic Braithwaite, was asked by James if he would say a few words but he declined, 'No, I haven't been briefed.' He listened to the other speeches intently. With his fluent Rus-sian, he was able to appreciate the lengthy speech by Sergei Klokhov, who emerged from the wings to seize the centre of the stage and the microphone too. With impeccable diplomacy, the Ambassador wore a fixed smile of apparent pleasure, though it was hard to tell what that

James Birch and Gilbert & George at the press conference, reminding me irresistibly of the Nuremberg Trials. Plainly guilty. Photo. Daniel Farson.

particular pleasure might be. His views on Gilbert & George remained conjecture but suspicions were confirmed when he admitted to James that they were not his 'cup of tea'.

His remoteness from the occasion suggested that he hated Gilbert & George's work, like most of the other English guests, including Trevor Fishlock from the *Daily Telegraph* and his wife who looked disapproving. James wondered if the Ambassador realised that his daughter's boyfriend had been featured in one of their pictures.

The Ambassador was polite when I photographed him, and evasive when I asked if he had any comment to make: 'No, not *yet*,' he replied

With Sir Roderic Braithwaite, the British Ambassador, to the immediate left, Sergei Klokhov seized the centre stage and microphone to give a lengthy discourse in Russian.   Photo. Keith Davey.

cautiously. Lady Braithwaite was more forthcoming – 'Frankly, I'm *foxed!*'

Surprisingly, the one person the Ambassador upset, however inadvertently, was George when he indulged in the usual small talk and asked him how long 'he had been in Moscow and what had he been doing. 'What on earth does he think I've been doing?' George exclaimed afterwards. 'Sightseeing?'

I had the nerve to introduce Sir Roderic to Dolly before he left. 'Your Excellency, may I have the honour to present Mrs Dolly J. Fiterman from Minneapolis.' He shot me a cool look and gave her Zandra Rhodes outfit a rapid appraisal, though he had the grace to shake her hand warmly although plainly bemused. 'Dolly is a friend of our Prime Minister,' I explained, and Dolly rose to the occasion as she described her recent visit to Downing Street and how kind Mrs Thatcher and

THE RUSSIAN REACTION

Denis had been to her while the Ambassador listened with a new respect. As he left Sir Roderic gave me an uneasy grin.

More than 1,000 people came to the Opening. As soon as the ritual of the speeches was over they swarmed into the rooms and Gilbert & George were pinioned into a corner as Russians jostled for their autographs in the splendid catalogues whose black-market value was increasing by the minute.

The exhilaration could be seen on their faces, especially of the young – there were even children present. Also the rich and famous: Tania Kolodzei with a personal collection of more than a thousand works of Russian art, and Francesca Thyssen with Sergei Klokhov in hot pursuit.

I recognised the eager faces of strangers invited by Gilbert & George in the course of the week, including the Mexican who could not understand a word of English.

There was a sense of occasion, an infectious excitement as if an event was taking place which would be seen as important in the future. Young Russians I spoke to confirmed that they regarded this as a turning point in the history of art, something entirely new. A typical reaction came from a young English admirer who told Gilbert & George, 'Every time I see your work I feel alive.'

'Mikhail Mikheyev recorded some of the Russian responses:

'Fantastic. Come more often!'

'Thank you for a new vision of the world.'

'Thank you for a spiritual celebration.'

'Thank you for the humanity, directed not only at the educated.'

'I'm fired with admiration!' (student aged sixteen)

'I really like art. Art is our life. Goodbye and thank you.' (student aged nine)

Mikhail explains: 'This is not an approximate summary of the audience's reaction but factual material. Out of every five written replies, four would be full of praise. Even if one can doubt the sincerity of art bureaucrats it is difficult to envisage hypocrisy in children. During less than four weeks of showing, the exhibition was seen by no fewer than 3,000 people each day. I do not think it left anyone indifferent.'

The Soviet art critics found the spiritual quality which Mikhail Mikheyev has referred to:

'The Moscow exhibition became another milestone for another of Gilbert & George's sacred concepts on which their work is based.' (Bespaslova, *Pravda*)

THE RUSSIAN REACTION

'Their art warns of the possible catastrophe and its inevitability if people do not listen to the voice of reason, do not become more generous, purer and more charitable.' (Han-Magomeda, *Izvestia*)

Mikhail continues, 'It would of course be unfair to say that the Gilbert & George exhibition had total success. It seems that the position of an average Moscow consumer differs little from that of a London one – in both cases intellectual apathy is replaced by a pose. Perhaps the Moscow consumer can be marked out by his greater severity in passing judgement, as for more than a century unenlightenment and narrow-mindedness were considered good taste.'

Here are some adverse responses:

'Corruption of the people.'

'Keep it to yourself in the USA.'

By some radar instinct, the swelling crowd at the Opening sensed the second that the doors would swing open to Gilbert & George's party below, and poured through them like a revolutionary mob after vengeance, though their objective here was food and drink. The security guards watched helplessly as gatecrashers pushed past without producing invitation cards, while the violinist from the Kolida restaurant greeted the artists with the Georgian wedding march, a joke attributed to Sergei Klokhov that went unnoticed at the time.

Tables were cleared as if by locusts, but I noticed that thirst preceded hunger with Russians drinking three glasses of champagne simultaneously, difficult though that may sound. Surprisingly, 162 bottles of French champagne – supplied through the British Embassy although provided by Gilbert & George and the d'Offay Gallery – were drained within ten minutes. No one seemed to object to the gatecrashers; after all, they appreciated the party as much as anyone. It was a great if short-lived success.

As for the exhibition, this was a triumph.

CHAPTER ELEVEN

PROFESSIONAL PARANOIA

I had been startled by the sudden appearance in the afternoon of Andrew Brown who flew in from Riga to attend the Opening, and had toured the exhibition with 'one of the heads of the KGB', or so he claimed, before it was open to the public.

I knew him from Scotland, where he is the director of the adventurous 369 Art Gallery, and invited him to appear on *Gallery* the previous autumn when he proved so effective that we asked him to stay a further night in Bristol and take part in a second programme. He proved wild, exuberant company, so I was delighted to see him in Moscow. Less so, however, when he announced that he was reviewing the exhibition for the *Mail on Sunday* with whom I had a personal association having worked for the paper for over a year as their television critic. When he told me he had just phoned through his story, I felt the chill of rivalry, especially as I had been assured that it was virtually impossible to phone London from the hotel, as he had done. Instead, I had gone to the offices of British Airways and filed my own story by fax. Until Andrew Brown's arrival I was well pleased (too well pleased) with my account of Gilbert & George in Moscow; now my professional hackles stirred as I recognised a competitor who might outscoop me. The deadline for the review section of the *Sunday Telegraph* was Thursday evening, while it was still possible to phone a news item to the *Mail on Sunday* as late as Saturday morning, so he had the advantage. My situation was reminiscent of the Hollywood cliché of the old hand threatened by the young upstart who has no compunction in breaking the rules in order to win the game – I was Edward G. Robinson.

After we left the exhibition hall for the buffet dinner at the Union of Artists I began to see Andrew Brown as a man determined to outsmart me, ignoring the fact that he had not even enquired what I was doing in Moscow. Even this indifference was vexing.

The last I remember of that evening was being hit by a woman in a red dress because I rejected her advances, and Brown's voice ricocheting across the room as he demanded of Gilbert, 'Why are you a paedophile?' Normally I'd have laughed. Then I flinched as I heard Gilbert's merry reply, 'Why shouldn't people love their children!' spoken with lovely, disarming laughter – yet a remark which could look terrible in the coldness of print. Gilbert looked towards me as if to say 'But this is *mad*!'

Gilbert told me he was aghast when he woke. 'Oh God! I didn't say fathers should fuck their children, did I?'

I was irritated when I woke for I thought it was six, until I realised my watch was upside down and it was twelve. Reflecting that obliteration by vodka is preferable to the fits and starts of semi-sobriety, I returned to harsh reality with the recollection of Andrew Brown's question and Gilbert's jaunty response.

First of all, I re-read my own story and though I was reassured, I knew that Andrew Brown's would be sensational if he had phoned through his confrontation of the night before: BRIT ARTIST RECOMMENDS CHILD LOVE TO SOVIETS.

I need hardly state that Andrew Brown would not have been so irresponsible, but I was a victim of professional paranoia, aggravated by the thought that my feature might not have reached London at all due to some technical fault on the part of the fax, a machine which still seemed too miraculous to be relied on. I phoned Mrs Fishlock in Moscow who was kind enough to telex a brief news item for the front page of the *Sunday Telegraph* which was still to go to press: CANVAS OF CHANGE IN ARTISTIC MOSCOW was the headline the sub-editors gave it – 'The Gilbert & George Exhibition in Moscow has caused a sensation with a greater attendance than that for the Francis Bacon show two years ago. Young Russians are especially enthusiastic, seeing the young modern British artists as a turning point in the history of art.'

That afternoon, still tormented by doubt, I risked a phone call to London and got through immediately.

'Yes, we received your little feature,' Richard Addis reassured me.

Little feature! This sounded ominous until he continued, 'The news item you telexed this morning.'

'Ah, that!' I said with relief. I longed to ask if he thought the main feature was everything he hoped for and more, but settled lamely: 'Then everything's all right?'

'Yes. Our picture department had a problem with the photographs [which I had sent by air on Wednesday] but they've sorted it out.' My heart sank again, what could have gone wrong? 'Nearly all the shots of Gilbert & George were head and shoulders only – legless.' I thought of saying, 'If you thought they were legless you should have seen the photographer,' but decided this might be unwise and kept silent. 'Anyhow,' he continued, 'we found one which was all right.'

Impetuously, I mentioned that the *Mail on Sunday* hoped to run a story too – realising too late that this was a mistake.

'You mean they're going to run a similar story tomorrow?' the voice was sharper.

'Yes. But I don't believe the writer even spoke to Gilbert & George personally. Just an art review.'

'That's all right then.'

Yet I put the phone down with a slight disappointment and the nagging anxiety that my camera might have developed a fault, which I would only be able to confirm when I saw the photographs on my return. In fact they were perfectly all right with ample shots of Gilbert & George, legs and all.

On Saturday night the British Council gave their dinner party, one of the less gracious occasions I have attended, with the irony that it was being held to placate Gilbert & George.

Though members of the Union of Artists were conspicuously absent, Klokhov himself turned up with his girlfriends.

The Georgian restaurant proved unsympathetic, with some of the nastiest food I ate in Russia and service of such indifference that it suggested that the British Council were not their favourite customers.

In due course we were treated to the obligatory British Council speech, which had all the fumbling platitudes of Wilfred Hyde White in *The Third Man*. The speaker said that he had been travelling with some minister or other which was why he had not actually seen the exhibition though he heard that it was very good and congratulated everyone for he knew how much work was involved and was sorry the British Council had not been able to help but they were so understaffed … and so on and so on.

A pall had fallen on the room after his admission that he had not seen the exhibition. No excuse was valid. 'He should have lied,' Gilbert told me afterwards. 'People had flown in from all over the world to see it, from Belgium, Italy, Holland, America and Germany – and the man from the British Council could not even bother to see it.

'Would they have been so against it if the art had been bad? It's only because we shocked the knickers off the natives!'

The Council's man had the wit to realise that his speech was humiliating in the circumstances and sat down reddening visibly in total silence until Sergei Klokhov got up and pointed out that inadequate acknowledgement had been given to the d'Offay Gallery.

The man from the Council protested that he had indeed expressed his admiration for Mr d'Offay, who was sitting beside him, and anyhow this went without saying. Silence.

Then, to everyone's consternation, George rose slowly and tapped his glass with such an impassive yet severe expression that I tensed myself, wondering what he was going to do, knowing how he detested speeches. Did he feel it was his duty to criticise the Council? Was he going to issue a writ?

Instead he announced, 'I have some very important news – it is Rudi Fuchs's birthday!' At this the tension broke and the room dissolved in uproar as we sang *Happy Birthday dear Rudi!* at the tops of our voices, followed by a solo rendition of the little-known second verse by Dolly Fiterman. After deafening applause, the British Council man departed, and to do him justice he looked suitably embarrassed.

'The way the British Council treat people is rotten,' said Stainton. 'They should treat people better if they're paid to represent them.'

In the event, my fears over Andrew Brown's 'scoop' proved groundless. His review did not appear in the *Mail on Sunday* while mine was featured in the *Sunday Telegraph* with the photograph I had taken underneath the gigantic statue of the Soviet worker and the peasant girl clutching their hammer and sickle. (With a bizarre turn of the circle, I succeeded Andrew Brown as Arts Correspondent for the *Mail on Sunday* in October 1990.)

I knew nothing of this at the time, but a copy of the *Sunday Telegraph* happened to be in the plane on the flight back to London on Sunday afternoon, and Jill Ritblat wrote to me that 'it was passed around the plane several times'.

Then someone turned the page and saw the announcement of Peter Fuller's death in a car accident. His chauffeur-driven car had overturned, his neck had been broken, his son was hurt, and his wife, who was expecting their second child, miscarried. It was unrelieved tragedy with the brutal irony that his father-in-law knew that Peter was overworked and persuaded him to be driven by someone else to make sure of the family's safety.

PROFESSIONAL PARANOIA

Since his death, Peter Fuller has been acclaimed as the finest British art critic of his time, and an editor of undeniable brilliance of *Modern Painters*. The warmth of the obituaries revealed an unexpected admiration towards this rather private man, even from those he opposed. He was antagonistic to Gilbert & George but had more in common with them than he realised.

One of Fuller's last written declarations began with the statement: 'If there is one thing I find as distasteful as Thatcherism, it is anti-Thatcherism: recently, of course, there has been a lot of it about. Margaret Thatcher's detractors on the Left persistently characterise her not as a political figure with whose policies they dissent, but rather as someone odious, tyrannical and even evil.'

With admirable candour, the former Marxist condemned the extremes of the Left. 'Looking back, I cannot comprehend how I, and so many others of at least reasonable intelligence, ever gave such stuff the time of day.'

As good critics should, yet few do, Peter Fuller had the ability to change his mind.

Peter Fuller appeared on *Gallery* when it was transmitted at six-thirty on Saturday, 12 May, a few hours after he had been killed. HTV were unaware of his death, and so the programme went ahead.

There is an additional and brutal irony: one week later Peter Fuller was due to give a lecture in Chicago to the 1990 International Art Exposition. The title was *Goodbye Andy Warhol, Farewell Gilbert & George*.

CHAPTER TWELVE

'WHAT A JOLLY PROCESSION!'

Was our Moscow experience exceptional, or did it seem so to me because of the novelty? I have no doubts. Apart from the excitement surrounding the exhibition, we arrived in Moscow at a crucial turning-point in the city's history. This was self-evident but it proved overwhelming on the first of May.

James, Judy, Keith Davey and myself stayed behind. Keith had to complete his coverage of the exhibition, and the rest of us stayed especially for the May Day celebrations. An acquaintance in a Bideford pub (who knew nothing about it whatsoever) had warned me to be there: 'Something is bound to happen. After Lithuania, Gorbachev *must* put on a display of force to make them realise he is still the boss.' This was idle bar-talk, but I have wondered since if it started a chain reaction, for I told the features editor of the *Sunday Telegraph* that 'there could be trouble', and Trevor Fishlock, their man in Moscow, advised me later that he had been told there could be trouble. At the same time, he disillusioned me, for I had assumed – like the man in the pub – that the first of May was the day of strength with marching soldiers, tanks and rockets grinding through the Red Square, while the Soviet leaders took the salute from the plinth over Lenin's tomb. Such occasions had been used frequently to daunt the West with images of power, as well as the Soviet people.

He explained that there are two May Days; the military parade taking place on the ninth. The first of May is devoted traditionally to athletic girls in gym-slips, twirling ribbons to the sound of music.

Not this time. Not on 1 May 1990.

I joined James and Judy downstairs, in the lugubrious lobby of the Ukraine, around ten am, hoping we had not left it too late in our

Everything I hoped for but did not expect, finding myself opposite Gorbachev, who stood on the plinth above Lenin's tomb. Wearing a hat, he is in the centre, to be joined a few moments later by Gabriel Popov, the new Mayor of Moscow. James said we should have carried a placard of our own. 'Down with the Poll Tax'.

Photo. Keith Davey.

attempt to reach the Red Square. We took a taxi, with the usual red-and-white flourish of Marlboro, and sped along the massive, empty motor-way towards the Red Square until we were stopped by the militia. After attempting several side-turnings, our driver gave up and we joined the people who were making their way on foot, with all the fun of spectators heading for the big parade. Soon the street was lined with soldiers, very definitely 'at ease', standing awkwardly, unarmed and unkempt. As we reached the Alexander Gardens below the walls of the Kremlin – *Kreml* means fortress – we found the broad street filled with a procession of men and women, old and young, carrying banners and different-coloured flags. Some were wearing ethnic costumes in the tradition of the first of May.

As we approached Red Square, the roads were lined with soldiers who refused to let us out, which was why we were swept along with the demonstration.   Photo. Keith Davey.

'What a jolly procession!' I exclaimed.

We reached the National Hotel, where we arranged to meet Keith, and could see up the hill towards the Red Square, crowded with people, with a vast poster of Lenin across the road with his hand raised as if to say 'Hi there!'

The two parallel roads seemed choked by crowds and we wondered what to do. James said we might gain a distant view from an upstairs window of the hotel. Exasperated by our indecision, and the acceptance that it was impossible to get nearer, I noticed that a group of people were moving forward and we were able to head in their direction, though the surrounding streets were cordoned off.

Suddenly, miraculously, we found ourselves in the 'jolly' procession, led by a priest carrying a banner with the white relief of the crucified Christ. I ran ahead to photograph him, followed by the others, and then looked round for a place on the pavement where we could

A photograph cannot convey the din: the blare of martial music, and the loudspeaker used by a man behind me who yelled his demand: 'Gorbachev, go!' so deafeningly that a woman near me held her ears against the noise – and possible danger.   Photo. Keith Davey.

walk alongside for it seemed presumptuous to stay as part of the procession. Impossible. The road into the Red Square was lined with soldiers who refused to let us through. We were swept along into the Red Square, into the very heart of Moscow's May Day, an opportunity I had not dared to expect. Within moments, or so it seemed, we came to a halt exactly opposite Lenin's tomb with Gorbachev among the line of leaders on the plinth, unmistakeable in spite of his grey hat – or because of it – with the new Mayor, Popov, beside him, whom I recognised from a newspaper photograph. And then all hell broke loose.

As you may have suspected, but in my naivety I did not, the jolly procession was a demonstration of Lithuanians and members of other Soviet States, like the Ukraine, who were demanding their independence. Like it or not, we were now a part of them, and we were trapped. Behind us, over GUM, soared the three gigantic faces of Marx, Engels and Lenin, dwarfing the crowds in the long immensity of the Square, with the tiny relief of Christ in contrast just a few yards away; on the other side lay Lenin's tomb; and all around us lines of plain-clothed police, the equivalent, apparently, of our Special Branch, kept us separate. They stared at us with unconcealed though phlegmatic dislike, apparently unarmed until we noticed the truncheons. Standing side by side, no one was allowed to pass through them.

This was handled superbly. If there had been trouble we could have been contained and isolated instantly. For several alarming, thrilling minutes it looked as if there must be trouble – 'something is sure to happen' – for there we were, directly in front of the podium, facing a line of the most powerful men in the Soviet Union, and the demonstrators seized this astonishing opportunity and erupted. A man next to me shouted at the top of his voice, his face contorted, while another, with a loudspeaker, led them in a chant, louder and fiercer every time.

'Do you speak any English?' I asked a man who was plainly not a demonstrator.

'Just a little.'

'What are they shouting?'

'They are shouting "freedom!" – they are telling Gorbachev to go. There has been nothing like it in our history before, nothing like it.' He wiped his face to conceal his emotion.

As the din increased, the nervous young policeman facing me developed a tic and soon his cheeks were fluttering like birds. On the plinth opposite, we could see Gorbachev drumming his fingers, unsmilingly, and all the time the Red Square was filled with the deafening sound of martial music which may have been intended to reassure yet seemed to exacerbate the drama. I looked at those around us; not all were demonstrators: a young Russian carried his child on his shoulders, waving a balloon and a small red flag. I noticed two or three cameramen, though I could not see anyone from British television, and one of them allowed me to climb on his tiny ladder to photograph the plinth and Gorbachev above the heads of the police in front of me. Altogether, we were enclosed in an area the size of half a football pitch and I suspect that a serious mistake had been made in letting the demonstration come to rest, when it should have been moved on.

The four of us turned to each other, smiling, elated, scarcely scared, for we knew there was nothing we could do if something went wrong such as a misjudged firecracker. When I took that photograph from the top of the ladder, I realised how easy it would be to shoot Gorbachev with a false zoom-lens, and though he must have known this he stood there with admirable unconcern. In such a situation, a dissident would be proud to risk his life.

Suddenly Gorbachev's patience was exhausted: he gave a sign with his fingers, and the leaders descended some steps and disappeared. They had endured enough. I learnt later that Gorbachev had given the order beforehand – 'No violence' – but it had proved a shocking disillusionment.

The demonstration was over and we poured down the far end of the Red Square, with no alternative but to follow the dispersing crowds, and noticed the water tanks with their hoses, and armed soldiers lined up below St Basil's in readiness for trouble. It took hours walking past cordoned streets we were not allowed to enter, towards the suburbs, until we found a taxi which took us a round-about direction to the hotel owned by Armand Hammer. Relaxing over vodka, we were still in a state of shock.

'My God, that was thrilling.' I looked around us at the absurd decorative clock, the forests of foliage, and the lifts that shot upwards like rockets, and thought aloud – 'We must have switched channels. We're in *Dallas!*'

That night, after fireworks shot across the sky, I drove past the Kremlin to find it all lit up, a fairyland of walls and towers with the garish colours of the onion domes of St Basil's. A large door in a gateway was half open, beckoning one to enter this dream after the harsh reality of the morning.

What had happened? Who had won? The ethnic demonstrators had made their protest but Gorbachev had allowed them to do so. In the middle of the night I woke up and knew I had witnessed a special moment in Soviet history. It was hardly comparable to the Kerensky Revolution which my father witnessed in Petrograd, and its significance was exaggerated afterwards out of all proportion by the Western press, but it was *thought* to be significant – and that was just as damaging to Gorbachev.

Western experts in their haste compared the demonstration to the one in Bucharest which marked the downfall of Ceauşescu. That was a wild distortion, but Soviet television conceded that the occasion had been spoilt by a few people who behaved 'incorrectly'.

I flew to Tblisi early the next morning, unaware of the rumpus in the Western world though suspecting I had witnessed the last of the first of May.

CHAPTER THIRTEEN

POST-MORTEM ON MOSCOW

There is a depression of spirit, bordering on a desperation, gripping the nation which never appeared in even its darkest totalitarian days. It is a blackness that goes far beyond the crumbling economy.

Harry Edgington from Moscow, *Daily Mail*, 25 September 1990

To take as much as possible from the State and give it back to the people.

The declared aim of Stanislav Shatalin, September 1990

On 2 May, James and Judy flew back to London, and later to New York, to join Gilbert & George who had stopped overnight at Fournier Street – 'to change our knickers' as Gilbert explained. With a stamina which was stoic so soon after Moscow, Gilbert & George went to New York *twice* for the openings of *three* exhibitions: at the Hirsch and Adler, the Robert Miller, and Sonnabend galleries, of 'Postcard Pieces' and new work.

'I assume,' I asked, 'that 1990 is the busiest year of your lives?'

'Certainly!' said George, with a lift of the eyebrows to indicate that it was inconceivable to think otherwise.

I missed out on this American jamboree, unaware that Gilbert & George wanted to include me, along with Troy, Stainton, James and Judy, but assumed that I knew New York all too well and might have been bored. Bored! The capitalistic contrast to the vanishing Communistic dream would have been fascinating.

To add to the disappointment, James regaled me with accounts of amazing dinner parties, a late-night visit to a dangerous club filled with six-foot negroes and Hispanic men on drugs, and a respectable outing to Stainton's sister in the Bronx for tea. Gilbert, who seems to relish bad behaviour vicariously, told me that George went missing in the hotel after their visit to the nightclub, and was found just in time as he tried to climb out of their window on the sixteenth floor. Stainton told me, 'You should have been there. You would have enjoyed it so much. Every time is different.'

Yet I was not too distressed. Though I should have welcomed the contrast of New York, I was anxious not to dissipate my experience of Moscow for this was unique. In New York it would have been tempting to explore on my own, to seek out recommended bars and restaurants, to look up former friends or strangers with treacherous letters of introduction – to stray. In Moscow there was no such temptation; the experience was inviolate.

It was after my return to London that I realised the full extent of the deep and different impressions Moscow made on us.

Stainton was shocked. 'What I've seen made me really ill inside. I felt so sorry for the people there – there's not much they can do. It's so bleak. Terrible to spend so much money on arms and so little on people. I would not like to go back.'

Keith Davey felt that it was all 'a grand façade', yet decaying behind the scenes. Bridges and buildings propped up with permanent scaffolding like a film set – all right from the front, a disaster at the back. But the scale of the boulevards was astonishing, twice as wide as the M25 motorway with six lanes of traffic in each direction.

'That May Day in Red Square is etched on to my memory for ever. I can admit now that I was quite worried at the time and you seemed so calm. If I had been alone I would not have gone into the Square and I would have missed the experience of a lifetime.'

Raymond O'Daly relaxed with such a vengeance after hanging the show that he woke the next morning in Leningrad. 'It was very beautiful but scary for I was there without a visa and didn't know how to get back. I discovered you have to book for the train ten days in advance. Luckily I had my passport and I went to the station anyhow. Each section of the train has a guard and each one said "No" and moved me on to the next. My God, I thought, I'm not going home. Finally one guard nodded as I tried to bribe him, but it was terrifying for I didn't know if the train would stop and I'd be chucked off.'

Raymond's companion in his carriage was a further cause for alarm; a former soldier in the Afghan war still suffering from the trauma. He gave Raymond accounts of his hand-to-hand, knife-to-knife combat, and how he was better trained than the man he killed, which was why he killed him. He described his emotions graphically – the guilt and the pouring sweat at the moment of death. 'His prize was the other man's machete. Luckily he was unable to find it on the train. However, he gave me a lesson in killing – the green nose – simply smash a bottle and put it in someone's face. He demonstrated this with a green bottle and stopped inches from my nose. It was scary.

'Every day I think about this dreadful, shocking country – it still makes nightmares for me, with visual images of hardship. Everyone said it was like going to the moon, and I remembered Buzz Aldrin's description – 'magnificent desolation'. That could be said of Moscow too. But it heightened my awareness of life. It made me aware of my mortality – a very funny feeling, almost indescribable.'

Julian Cole, another visitor to Moscow, where he was displayed in the picture *See* (1987), came there to continue a film he was making on Gilbert & George and their work. He had shot video footage of their AIDS exhibition and four hours of interview, and hoped to secure money for a full-length documentary. 'Unfortunately this did not happen, but nevertheless I decided that this trip had to be recorded and took myself and a small High Video Camera. However there has been little interest from television and all twenty hours of footage remain unedited.'

Julian Cole was one of the disillusioned, as he wrote to me afterwards: 'I felt how I sometimes feel when visiting a small country town. Perhaps this is slightly arrogant but it is as if I have had access to huge areas of knowledge and experience that they have been denied. This could be seen in all kinds of ways, especially talking to people involved with art – Western art has moved through so many trends and concepts which they have not yet discussed. I noticed this most of all when watching people look at Gilbert & George's work during the opening of the exhibition; much the same type you would see at the Hayward but these people seemed confused by the work, much of which had explicit homoerotic imagery, and in Russia people are not used to thinking about, let alone discussing, sexuality. In the West this has been on the agenda for twenty years and huge strides have been made in every aspect of liberating 100 years of prejudice. In Russia I felt they had been denied the opportunity to think and discuss this and so many other issues that the intellectuals of the art world in the West would take for granted. It was a unique insight into how people might have reacted to such issues in England in the 1940s. They often seemed desperate to talk about such issues to get some knowledge of where progressive thinking is at, but they did not have the vocabulary or ease to really engage in discussion. There was still a nervousness, despite Glasnost, to talk openly so one ended up getting official-speak. Everyone was desperate to talk to you, wanting knowledge of what we were thinking, which is not surprising considering that they are unable to travel. [This restriction is being lifted rapidly; in 1989 two and a half million people received visas to travel abroad, twenty times more than in 1968.]

'Every minute you spent talking to them seemed hugely significant to them and consequently very exhausting. They sensed what I am saying here and this had the effect of them wanting to impress on me that they were not so different – that they were thinking about things that people in the West think about. We were their guests and they went out of their way to make us feel at home, but this was an impossible task and they knew it. So this seemed in some ways strangely pathetic, they knew they were failing and that we were looking down at them. So they got drunk.

'I did feel sorry for them – they were all very bright and ambitious people in the prime of their lives desperately trying to make the best of things. It was not the lack of material things but the lack of access to ideas, opinions, thinking, which seemed to be the real crime of what Communism had been.'

Though I suspect the Muscovites deplore the lack of food as much as the access to ideas, they are a *free* people today – whatever that word means – though the crime of Communism which Julian Cole refers to has left them in a state of shock, amnesiacs who dare not remember the full horror. Like soldiers who survived the trenches in the First World War and were never the same again, a Russian would have had to be slightly mad in the first place to emerge from Communism completely sane.

We still have no concept of the full extent of that horror which makes even Hitler's genocide seem moderate: the destruction of the peasant system in the Republics, the confiscation of property which destroyed the *kulaks* so that no one was left with anything of value, the deportation of children never to be seen again, the famine in the Ukraine which starved ten million people to their deaths, the loss of all dignity – how could the Russians not be embittered now? The humiliation that continues is inconceivable to us, and made me feel humiliated too, with empty Western beer cans as objects of desire, and eggs at £2 each as I write this now. Communism may be lifting like a morning mist but there are still corners where it lingers. In Minsk an English friend who was marrying a Russian girl visited his future in-laws to find them distressed, having just been questioned by the KGB who informed them that their daughter was known to be consorting with a Westerner and had been declared 'an enemy of the people'. And this took place in 1990! Admittedly the police laughed this off when they spoke to the Englishman, and he was strong enough to do so too, but their surveillance car remained below his window.

In Moscow, that deeply disillusioned city, there is a terrible anxiety if no longer fear – but I felt betrayal round the corner.

Conversely, the effort in maintaining the façade has led to a desperate gallantry exemplified by the stoicism of the Muscovites as they queued for something we would spurn, drably dressed, with the bloated looks which accompany hunger and the need to stuff yourself with bread and potatoes. Stoicism or resignation? Probably both.

Particularly sad were the paucity of the luxuries and foibles we rely on. I heard that when lavatory paper was virtually unobtainable, Muscovites who had some wore a roll of the coloured paper like a scarf in order to show off. When soap powder was equally scarce, women carried empty cartons as handbags in order to impress their neighbours. Though vanity may be denied, a wistful pride remains and Anthony d'Offay told me that when he was unable to get a taxi he stopped a car, as we had been advised, offering the driver the ubiquitous packet of Marlboro: 'But the man, who drove me back to the hotel, handed them back. Unbelievably proud – incredibly touching.'

James Birch loved Moscow, though, in retrospect, he is beginning to wonder if there were undercurrents he failed to notice at the time. A moment of doubt occurred after the British Council's party, returning to the Ukraine after the inevitable detour to the Belgrade Two bar to notice a sinister-looking man in a leather coat standing on the steps as if he was waiting for them. He followed James and Judy into the lobby and they stopped to let him pass on the way to the lift. As they took their own lift to the nineteenth floor, they burst into helpless laughter at their absurdity in thinking they were being followed. The doors opened – and there was the man in the leather coat! James is still not sure ...

Troy thought Moscow was the most beautiful city he had visited. 'Beyond the architectural splendour are the amazing people: the Russians' faces are unique, saying more about life than a lengthy novel. Every line, every wrinkle tells of a chapter in that person's life. Visitors to Moscow always remark that few of the city's inhabitants smile; I believe this isn't a demonstration of unhappiness but a sort of rebellion against the amount of inane smiling so common to Western countries.'

He hopes to return and live there for several months. 'Sure, the food is revolting and the corruption is widespread – I find that rather charming.'

Did the Moscow experience change us? There is no doubt of that. Raymond O'Daly told me that it proved a turning-point: 'You get infected by all the excitement. It had a momentum all its own. After that, everything was a bit boring.'

Returning to England he was offered a new job by the Flowers East Gallery in Hackney and accepted it, though he has since departed.

Judy Adam was a casualty of sorts, resigning from her top job at the d'Offay Gallery, where she had been instrumental in organising exhibitions by Lucian Freud and Joseph Beuys as well as Gilbert & George. Understandably, after fourteen years, Anthony d'Offay was reluctant to part with her and their severance was unhappy.

One of the collectors fell out of love with his friend – 'It may seem extraordinary, but when I saw him underneath a poster of Lenin, I realised what a small person he was!' Another Moscow casualty.

James Birch in particular has been transformed. During one of our late-night sessions in the Ukraine when truths were told, I accused him of being too modest for his own good. He was the vital catalyst between the two countries and deserved to benefit from the goodwill achieved.

'But I don't want to make anything out of it!' he persisted.

'In twenty years' time you may be sorry.'

As the least business-like person myself, this was colossal cheek, except that it is easy to recognise one's own deficiency in others. A healthy lack of ambition is rather attractive and I should have left him alone, especially as I know now that an iron will is concealed beneath the flopsy image. However, our talk seemed to galvanise him overnight, as if I had assumed the role of Dr Frankenstein.

Today James Birch is recognised as the indispensable link between the artist and the Russians, following the success of Gilbert & George's exhibition. David Hockney asked him to fly to Los Angeles in September to discuss an exhibition which may well be shown at the New Tretyakov Gallery late in 1991 or early in 1992 if conditions in Moscow do not prevent it. Personally, I believe that the Gilbert & George will be the last great exhibition in Moscow for several years to come.

As for myself, I have a puzzling sense of reprieve as if I have emerged from a long and serious illness.

Everyone benefits from new incentive, especially the solitary writer unless he has people around him whose judgement he relies on. As one grows older it is especially rewarding to make new friends whom you trust and whose company stimulates. Gilbert & George are life-enhancers but I have wondered about the special rapport which existed between us.

Could there be an affinity because George and I share the same birthday? Yet I feel an equal sympathy with Gilbert. They are the straightest people I know.

Perhaps the greatest gift one can ask of friends is loyalty and I have seen how loyal they are to those they trust, in spite of their mock lament that they have no friends.

Another gift is the opening of new horizons when so many people are a cul-de-sac. Gilbert & George opened horizons for all of us, literally so for myself, and especially for James, who returned to Moscow to dismantle the exhibition before taking the train to Kiev, as he described in a letter:

> Misha Mikheyev wants to take me to Kiev with the mission of giving Princess Anne and Mrs Thatcher a signed catalogue each from Gilbert & George. They are in Kiev for British Week which without a doubt would not have happened if it hadn't been for the Bacon show two years earlier.

> When Judy hears I have a ticket and not her, she is furious and determined to go to Kiev as well. Luckily, Marina gets her a ticket but her train is nine minutes before ours. Misha takes us to the station which is really rather beautiful with lots of hammer and sickles, red flags and symbols. The trains also have the same motifs. I was feeling v. excited at the prospect of travelling by train. Misha and I climb aboard. The train itself is v. comfortable and civilised with mattresses, pillows and towels (which is unfortunate as there was no water). The other people in our carriage were a colonel from the Red Army and a farm labourer called Yuri from the Ukraine. When the train started we all got out our food and drink. I bring out whisky, smoked salmon pâté and oat cakes from Scotland. The Colonel brought out a piece of paper with two spring onions, one piece of cheese, four slices of salami and a ½-gallon petrol-can of vodka, and Misha the same.

> The female guard who was enormous with one gold tooth in her head was surprised I was on this Soviet train and not on Intourist. Misha explained I was on a mission to see Princess Anne in Kiev, she was v. impressed and shook my hand. Yuri

who was drunk by this point kept kissing her hand. She liked this and wanted Yuri to stay with her in her private room that night. Yuri got so pissed in the end that he fell asleep though singing all night long.

The guard woke us up two hours earlier than usual because of Yuri's mistake in not going to see her. During the journey stories were exchanged and the view from the window was one continuous birch forest. When it came to eating my food they were suspicious but soon liked it and gobbled it up within minutes.

It saddened me to think that the only time strangers speak to each other in Russia is on a train because they know they will never see each other again.

When we arrived in Kiev we had lunch of Chicken Kiev (reconstructed chicken) and headed off for the opening of the British Art Show to present the catalogues to Anne and Mrs Thatcher. This was abortive for we were told we would have to send them to their private secretaries in London.

It is *incredible* to think that Gorbachev received a signed catalogue and must have been impressed as an article came out on the front page of the leading Moscow newspaper about Gilbert & George the next day. Also that your review in the *Sunday Telegraph* was the only one to appear in an English newspaper when there were so many in Moscow publications.

After two days we went back to Moscow, sad to leave Kiev, which is v. beautiful rather like Paris or other mid-European cities before the war.

I had flown south to Georgia on the morning after May Day, travelling by Aeroflot where someone had been sick in the understandably empty seat beside me. I appreciate that readers may complain that my experiences in the Caucasus had nothing to do with Gilbert & George, and logically this is undeniable.

Yet for me this conclusion was crucial. Just as the journey to Kiev provided an extension for James, the Caucasus were my fulfilment. And without the Gilbert & George exhibition in Moscow this would have been denied me.

CHAPTER FOURTEEN

THE TRAGEDY OF KHASSAUT – A POSTSCRIPT TO MOSCOW

After the grimness of Moscow, Tblisi was airy, spacious – free. As if I had left a dungeon and entered the light. There were green trees and a cheerful river bustled through the town, with views of the distant Caucasus beyond. There was food in the shops – at a price – and no queues.

The contrast confirmed that I was no longer in Russia but in Georgia, one of the other fifteen Soviet states. Russian is scarcely spoken in Tblisi and the Russians are no longer so welcome after the massacre in 1989 when twenty people, mainly women, were killed outside the government headquarters in the Rustaveli Boulevard which is marked today by commemorative stones and flowers, with Lenin's statue dominating the square at the far end, an arm outstretched; but for how long? Stalin's has already toppled. In the free election of October 1990 the Communists were defeated, and I gather that Lenin's statue has been toppled too.

Conversely, foreigners receive the warmest welcome, though I needed a visa. That first evening I ate in the jolly basement restaurant, the Daryal, lined with large reproductions of the paintings by the Georgian primitive Pirosmani, and it was impossible to eat alone, indeed I had to be tactful as to which table I should join. Then there were constant toasts: 'To Georgia, the greatest country', 'To our families', 'To our children'. When I explained that I had no children, this was changed to 'Childhood friends' – and I toasted Anthony West with whom I had been at school at Abinger Hill, where I was the last headboy before we were evacuated to Canada. 'To Anthony Vest!' echoed the Georgians as I rose to my feet.

Two days later I flew across the Caucasus on a radiant morning which meant that I could look down on every peak and valley far below, the most exhilarating flight of my life though it lasted little more than 30 minutes.

For the first time I experienced the spell of that mountain range, the snows tinged with pink from the rising sun. They are stupendous: twelve peaks higher than Mount Blanc with 125 miles of glaciers, ice and snow between Mount Kazbeck and Mount Elbrus, the highest at 18,784 feet. With their raging rivers and carved gorges, their primeval forests and remote valleys which were only accessible for a couple of months in the year, the Caucasus provided a refuge for alien tribes, outlaws and intellectual exiles since the beginning of civilisation until they were conquered by the Tsars and decimated by the Communists.

This massive chain, which separates Europe from Asia, runs for 650 miles from the Black Sea to the Caspian, yet they offer you constant solace once you have reached them and the feeling that part of you belongs there however far you have travelled. I am no mountaineer but I can appreciate the lure of mountains, and the Caucasus are *comforting*.

Now I began to understand their appeal to Lermontov, Tolstoy, and my father who described them in *Caucasian Journey*:

> In the spring of 1929 I set out to ride horseback over the Western Caucasus with Alexander Wicksteed, an old English eccentric who, for six years, had been trying to live like a Russian in Red Moscow. Our intentions were to get the first pair of horses in Kislovodsk, then to proceed by easy stages, camping out on the northern spurs of the Caucasus wherever we liked a place, or I found some good trout fishing; finally, to try and take our horses over the snow-clad Klukhor Pass (9,400 feet) and ride down beside the foaming river Kodor to the melon beds of Sukhuum on the shores of the Black Sea.
>
> Negley Farson

When I re-read these opening sentences, I did so with pride and yet dismay, for I was writing a travel book of my own and knew I could not emulate his prose. Persuading the Penguin Travel Library to reissue *Caucasian Journey* as a paperback in 1988, I read it yet again and realised that this is my favourite of all his books, though little known compared to *The Way of a Transgressor*, as fresh as a recent fall of snow, perfectly self-contained, combining the spontaneity of his notes in 1929 with the benefit of his contemplation twenty years later.

I yearned to follow in his footsteps and see the Caucasus for myself.

THE TRAGEDY OF KHASSAUT

At Mineralnye Vodi I was greeted by my Russian contact, Yuri, who waited anxiously on the tarmac for we had not met before. A charming young teacher of English, he spoke it perfectly and we were driven to Pyatigorsk by his father, a retired army officer, who had never spoken to a foreigner before.

Mineralnye Vodi means 'mineral waters' for this is a region of natural springs with four spas which were highly fashionable in the Tsarist days of the last century when they were considered the equal of Baden-Baden. As for the famed Narzan mineral water, my father wrote, 'A White Russian in Paris would give his last franc for a bottle of it. This had been a favourite drink of the wild mountain tribesmen long before a Russian ever set foot in the Caucasus. "The drink of heroes!" they called it. And they *bathed* in it for centuries. Some, it must have been, for the sheer delight in wallowing in such exciting stuff (it is the most amazing feeling); but most because of the ancient, and still held, belief in its magical qualities.'

These included a cure for venereal disease, as Wicksteed discovered when he shared a pool with two swarthy men who explained why they were there and showed him the evidence.

'Great God!' Wicksteed exclaimed. 'I won't feel safe for weeks!'

Over lunch at the Intourist Hotel with Mount Elbrus rising some 60 miles away, now seen from the other side, I outlined my plans to Yuri, disconcerted that it was impossible to order one of the 600 varieties of Caucasian wine and forced to drink a fierce Georgian cognac instead without the soothing benefit of mineral water. Even for me, this was punitive in the middle of the day.

'Why on earth can't I have some Narzan water to wash it down?'

'Because no one has asked for it before.'

Even here, the Russians (for I had left Georgia and was once again in Russia) had been bludgeoned by years of accepting 'Niet!' for an answer.

First I would go to Kislovodsk which presented no problem for this was Yuri's home; then to the Karachaite village of Khassaut, and as far beyond as possible. Yuri was enthusiastic though he doubted if such a journey was possible without a special permit.

The next morning I took a crowded tram to the station in Pyatigorsk (asking for the *Voxall* after our own Vauxhall) and stood in an equally crowded train to Kislovodsk as my father had done 60 years earlier. We crossed a countryside with lilac woods in blossom and women in headscarves hoeing their immaculate plots, and others sunbathing on the green banks in the spring sunlight. Extraordinarily satisfying. My father wrote of his elation somewhere in the Caucasus: 'It is seldom, as we get on, that one feels the

Though not a mountaineer myself, I can understand the lure of mountains, for every one is different. I have seen Ararat and have heard of the hostility of Everest. Surprisingly, in spite of their immensity, the Caucasus are comforting. My father captioned this photograph: 'Breaking camp – the morning this poor specimen of a Karachaite tried to leave us in the lurch.'

sudden unaccountable, bubbling happiness of youth. I had a burst of it as we sat there ...'

I had it too. Such happiness can hit you as hard in a crowded train as it can on a mountain. Also, the *awareness* of happiness which hardly occurs to one when young. I remembered the moment in Tolstoy's *The Cossacks* which I carried with me, along with Lermontov's sardonic masterpiece *A Hero of Our Times,* and the excitement of the cynical young officer, Olenin, when he sees the mountains for the first time appearing to 'run along the horizon, their rosy tops gleaming in the rays of the rising sun. All his Moscow recollections, his shame and his regrets, all his trivial dreams of the Caucasus, departed and never returned again. "Now it has begun!" a sort of triumphant voice said to him.'

My approach was mundane by comparison, but I sympathised with his elation: Now it has begun.

This was the contented village of Khassaut, which greeted my father in 1929. A grand house with a balcony and cupolas to the left, the mosque in the distance, for Karachaites were Muslim.

Photo. Negley Farson.

Yuri and his girlfriend met me at Kislovodsk and we walked down the hill past attractive shops into a main square with impressive old buildings and tea gardens beyond. With gracious flowerbeds and an absence of traffic, I was astounded to find myself in the most elegant town I had seen in Russia. Yet I knew that my father hated the place when he arrived there in 1929. The reason was simple and added to the excitement: he entered the Caucasus as the Bolsheviks were moving in with all their reforms, while I arrived as these policies were being discredited.

My father expected an echo of the watering place beloved by the Tsarist officers of the Army of the Caucasus and their women – 'a place of rendezvous, lovers' trysts, of picnics on horseback into the wild ravines of the mountains, of arched eyebrows plucked by pretty fingers; the mazurka, gold epaulettes – and duels.' His disillusionment was absolute:

Now all that was over. Romance was gone, beauty was dead. And Wicksteed and I, wandering around in our search for horses, felt as alien in that hostile existence as if we had been

This is Khassaut as I found it in 1990, photographed from the same position. Only fifteen houses are left. The base of the mosque lies in the distance, but the minaret has been destroyed. At least my father's photograph, which I carried with me, showed the few inhabitants how grand their home had once been. Ali, the Karachaite, is on the left of Yuri, the English teacher at Kislovodsk and my invaluable interpreter.

Photo. Daniel Farson.

invaders from another planet. The faces of even the old buildings had changed – and refused us admission. The Grand Hotel, the Park, etc, these had become the Red Stone, Red October, the Karl Marx Sanatorium, all reserved for responsible Communist Party workers – and no arched eyebrows plucked by pretty fingers or any bourgeois nonsense about being drowned in love for the factory lads and lassies (if such there were among that lot) who now inhabited them. Love had been put on a 'natural' basis; like an animal going on heat. It was about as unappetising and vexatious an atmosphere as I ever want to breathe. Even old Wicksteed, indefatigable champion of the proletariat, had to mutter as we stared at the odiously arrogant, happy, and hostile faces all staring at us, in the Narzan Gallery: 'This is a *beastly* place! Already ruined by tourists! I would not want to spend a night here even if we could stay!' I had to smile; that he should call his beloved Bolshevik 'tourists'!

My father's dislike seems excessive, but he had been covering the USSR for the *Chicago Daily News* and described the early part of 1929 as 'unquestionably the high point of the Revolution – the Russians were still human (as they will be again some day). In roving about Russia I had met Communist after Communist whose devoted self-sacrifice and zeal had aroused my envy.'

Now, after his 'long, lazy and hopeful trip', 1,800 miles down the rivers Moskva and Oka until they reached the Volga, he was furious to arrive in Kislovodsk and find the 'old boring Moscow atmosphere again: all the suspicions, and politically indoctrinated hates':

> It can be understood why the faces of the Narzan Gallery struck me as odiously happy: they were mutton, sheep. And their ignorance about the outside world was invincible. The clear streams, the snowy mountains, the deep pine and fresh beech forests, all the ever-new and radiant beauty of nature – these idiots, with their materialistic conception of life, would deny anything but utilitarian values: what they could get out of them. Staring at them, I thought that while the mountains themselves, the sheer rocks might defy them, the mountaineers could not: this spring of 1929 was probably the last when one could ride up among the tribesmen in the higher Caucasus and still be among free men ...

Delighted to be at variance with my father for once in my life, I asked Yuri to show me the places which had offended him. The Grand Hotel, where he was rejected, is now a sanatorium, an impressive, well-kept building on the corner of the main square. As for the detested Narzan Gallery which was built in 1894, the 'sheep' were still there and I joined them, 'odiously happy' too, in spite of a glass of the sulphurous water which may be health-giving but is undeniably foul like most drinks which are good for one, though the sparkling water from the natural springs proved pure and invigorating over the next few days.

Outside the Narzan Gallery, Yuri spoke to the 'bus lady' who sat beside a small table and handed out the tickets. After much shaking of heads, Yuri turned to me, his open face creased with worry: 'Big problems, Daniel.' Such a familiar phrase in Russia.

'There is no bus, Daniel, no car, and no foreigners can go without permit from the militia.' Even Yuri was used to accepting 'Niet!' for an answer, whereas I was damned if I was going to give up having travelled so far. We headed for the Intourist office in the Kavkaz Hotel (Kavkaz meaning Caucasus) where three plump Russian women polished their nails and added to their already formidable make-up with more mauve around the eyes.

Yuri explained. They bristled. Finally they yielded some shreds of information: 'Impossible. Everything closed.' Anyhow, we needed to ask Intourist in Pyatigorsk.

'Would you telephone them for us?' An outraged 'Niet!'

'Do you know the number?' Absolutely not; they glowered at such impertinence.

'Of course they do know,' said Yuri dejectedly as we left. 'They didn't want to tell us.'

'They remind me of the three monkeys,' I told him: hear nothing, say nothing, do nothing. 'Three baboons,' he corrected me.

And then we had our first piece of luck. Taking Yuri and his girlfriend to their favourite restaurant, a mock castle with individual caves on the outskirts of the town, I noticed that our taxi-driver seemed friendlier than the three baboons. Yuri agreed: 'I see his face. A trustworthy guy.'

'Then ask *him* if he will drive us to Khassaut.'

'To Khassaut!' Yuri echoed, never having gone so far before. 'Yes. I will try.'

'I will pay him well,' I added, resorting to that treacherous yet most persuasive argument. While I writhed in the back with impatience, they spoke interminably until Yuri turned round, his face bright with triumph. 'Amazing! Sasha says he will do it for us for 100 roubles.' As this was the equivalent of £10 it seemed negligible until I remembered that Yuri's salary is only 150 roubles a month.

'That is fine by me,' I agreed, trying not to sound dismissive. 'Well done, Yuri!'

'He is really surprised to find an Englishman here. He is being very hospitable.' Yuri's girlfriend embraced me: 'I'm so happy!' They had broken the curse of the downtrodden Russians, conditioned to that ubiquitous 'Niet!' as the irrevocable verdict. Sasha waited for us faithfully outside the Voxall on Monday morning and we set out in high spirits:

Dennis, the sleepy-eyed student in love with little Olga; Yuri; and Ali the Karachaite friend he had been trying to contact throughout the weekend. A 32-year-old mountaineer who was studying Spanish, Ali's company was indispensable, for the Karachaites are Mohammedan and like so many of the old Caucasian tribes they do not speak Russian. Apart from his usefulness as an interpreter for Yuri, Ali's face radiated good humour. I could not have wished for better companions.

The moment we left Kislovodsk the land was different. This was the land of 'water wet, grass green and mountains steep' as Wicksteed had described the Caucasus. We were entering a territory once inhabited by a score of tribes: the Kalmucks who came here in the thirteenth century with the grandson of Genghis Khan; their enemies, the Tchetchens; and the Karachaites who go back 2,000 years. In 1828, in the mountains at the far end of the Hurzuk valley (which I reached the following day), 500 Karachaites fought 20,000 Tsarist troops who won in the end and gave the best of the land to the Cossacks. In 1929 the Communists held out the promise that this land would be given back, issuing posters depicting a new dawn of tractors, waving wheat and happy men and women – Irritating posters!' wrote my father, who suspected that they were happier with their bullocks and handlooms and the skill of their saddle making, more than they would be with the tractor as slaves to a machine in some factory. If that happened, he feared they would lose 'real freedom'. As they did.

'Once Wicksteed and I had left Kislovodsk,' wrote my father in 1929, 'and crossed over the first mountain range, we found that our knowledge of Russian was no longer of any use to us. In the country of the Turco-Tartars we began to converse in sign language.'

Preparing their journey in Moscow, Wicksteed had traced a line from Kislovodsk to Mount Elbrus: 'If you go in there, you will find that "they" [the Communists] have not got much above 5,000 feet. There you will find the Caucasus as they used to be – the home of absolutely free men! And men of a fierce freedom such as you will find nowhere else in the world.' He sighed: 'At any rate – they *were*.' His reservation was justified as most of the tribes were scattered by the encroaching Soviets, traditions of centuries were shattered (the Khevsurs, descended from the Crusaders, wore chain-mail as late as the 1890s) though Ali believes there may be as many as 100,000 Karachaites surviving today. Though they are farmers rather than gypsies, they are viewed with suspicion by the Russians in Kislovodsk because they are Muslim. 'Not really antagonistic,' Yuri explained, 'but misunderstandings. Young Karachaites cause trouble when they're drunk and out of control. Some people think they are not intelligent and treat them arrogantly ...' He shrugged. 'But there are good people as well as bad people.' The few I met looked wild, wore beautiful high leather boots, and I felt you could trust them with your life if they had not taken it already.

We drove on past grazing cattle, goats, donkeys and the black sheep indigenous to Karachay. There had been a fall of snow overnight and as we went higher the road was obscured and I dreaded that we might have to turn back, but Sasha had no such doubts and we skidded on. 'I do not believe a better driver,' said Yuri.

We descended to green valleys where flocks of black sheep fed beside a river tended by a solitary shepherd as he would do day after day, possibly year after year. A few wild horses romped over the hills; smaller than most, these horses are among the finest and the Circassians among the most skilful riders, able to bend down from the saddle and pluck a wild flower as they pass.

We reached Khassaut at noon. Six hundred houses had greeted my father; instead we found a village in ruins with fifteen inhabitants. The 'main' street looked especially forlorn due to the single spindly television aerial, like one of those emaciated birch trees in Moscow, absurdly inapposite. Somehow, an electric cable has penetrated even this abandoned spot.

Throughout our journey, Ali had referred constantly to the photograph of Khassaut taken by my father and reproduced in the first edition of *Caucasian Journey*, but now he was confused.

I looked at the photograph again and then I looked around me. Where was the mosque? Where the fine houses? What on earth had happened?

It is a tragic story. The Karachaites have always been independent, regarding Karachay as an autonomous republic. They resisted the Tsar but resented their ultimate subservience to the Communists even more. When the Germans invaded the Caucasus in the last war and reached Kislovodsk, a leading Karachaite family presented the German general with a stallion, a saddle embroidered with silver, and a golden sabre. The Karachaites preferred the Germans to the Soviets. They were not forgiven. When the Germans left, many of the Karachaites went with them and made their way to America, while Stalin swept back with orders that Khassaut should be destroyed and the villagers given six hours to pack before they were deported to Siberia. Even for Stalin, this was a cruel revenge.

'Stalin punished the whole Karachaite nation,' Yuri translated, after

THE TRAGEDY OF KHASSAUT

Ali explained the cause of Khassaut's wretchedness today. 'It was so unfair. Stalin destroyed everything. He abolished private property though under Lenin our economy was doing well. Collectivisation destroyed our agriculture. And he exterminated free people like the Karachaites. This is why so little is known about their history, for Stalin destroyed their books as well – he did not want the nationalities to learn about their backgrounds. At last we can talk about it. Ali says you are the first to be interested.'

'When the soldiers moved in, couldn't some of the Karachaite men have fought them or escaped to the mountains?'

'How can you resist a machine-gun with a dagger?' Yuri replied.

Under Krushchev, the Karachaites were allowed to return to the Caucasus but by then not many were left.

Apart from one old man and two Karachaite farmers with fox-like grins and hats like curly wigs, there was no sign of life in Khassaut. Ali disappeared with the old man in the hope of learning news of a distant relative, returning in a few minutes with several headscarved peasant women who studied the photograph in *Caucasian Journey* with exclamations of astonishment.

Ali translated these to Yuri who told me, 'They say Bless you, Bless you! Thank the gentleman from England.'

'But why?' I could sense, yet not understand their excitement.

'For the first time they know what their village looked like.'

That was tremendously moving. Inadvertently I had brought them proof that Khassaut had once been a grand place, a village to be proud of. The few of us walked to the outskirts where my father took his photograph 60 years earlier, showing a splendid house on the left with cupolas and balustrades, with the minaret of the mosque rising in the distance. These were rubble now and took time to identify. Set in this sweeping valley beside the river with the snow peaks around us, Khassaut looked infinitely forlorn with so little of the former elegance left, just the ruins, a few shacks, and the still impressive though incongruous Culture Club built 100 years ago when every cornerstone was worth a lamb.

I could understand why the few remaining families welcomed this proof from the past – that their home had known dignity. Asking if they still observed the Muslim religion, Ali confirmed that they pray to Mecca four times a day and on special occasions travel to a mosque in some distant village, though he had no idea where this was.

Sitting on a bank near the well of bubbling Narzan water – at least Stalin had not been able to eliminate that! – I re-read my father's account of this borderline community in 1929:

Myself in a heavy black sheepskin coat, though not the true *burka* as worn by the shepherds to protect them from the cold, for that is worn back to front. I realise I look ridiculous, but that has never bothered me, though it might look better on a shepherd or a sheep.

THE TRAGEDY OF KHASSAUT

Picture these horsemen in a little mountain village of thatched stone houses, with a minaret like a stick of chalk standing up against the blues and greys of some nearby limestone crags, selling and buying horses, galloping down the main road after wandering cattle, reaching down at full gallop to pick from the ground one of their sheepskin hats which they had thrown there in mere bravado, rounding up the grey cattle, smoking, gossiping, lying flat on their faces in the warm sun – you have a perfect picture of Khassaut on a Sunday morning. Friday is the Mohammedan day of rest.

And like all good Mohammedans they were letting the women do all the hard work. Outside another stone and plaster house, on whose roof was already growing a good crop of grass, an old crone was weaving on a handloom. Another hag sat beside her spinning thread from a plummet-like spindle, which she set whirling with a sharp rub against her old leg. The Fates of the Karachaites – of what battles with the Cossacks of the line could these old women tell!

Those battles had known grandeur, even romance, with each side respecting the courage of the other. In the last century the Karachaites fought the Cossacks for months on end, and when they were forced to surrender they did so with honour. But as Yuri said, how could they resist the Communist machine-gun armed merely with a dagger?

Looking down from the position where my father took his photograph, Khassaut was dead. A beautiful black stallion imprisoned in an iron cage below me seemed symbolic, until Ali explained that sick animals were kept there to make it easier for the vet. So much for my fervid imagination. Yet the tragedy surrounding the village was unmistakeable.

My father was able to buy his horses in Khassaut and rode into the Caucasus for several spellbound weeks, leaving Wicksteed in Teberda, until he was forced back by the Klukhor Pass on the final stage of his journey.

My own Caucasian journey was tame by comparison, though I should not decry it. I had travelled in his tracks, albeit briefly and in comfort, and I had learnt the tragic fate of Khassaut. I believe my father would have been pleased that I had seen the Caucasus.

We drove back to Kislovodsk before darkness, a vast home-made cheese in the boot presented to me by the woman who had invited us into her home for the best meal I ate in Russia, with food I could actually taste, including a cool, refreshing sour milk which made feel physically better as I spooned it down, so pure I could sense my stomach thanking me with relief after the quantities of Georgian brandy forced down it over the past few days.

Yuri told me it would be dreadfully impolite if I refused the cheese, though I wonder how it would survive the journey home via Moscow and Istanbul. (I solved this by giving it to his mother.)

We passed the same shepherd and it seemed that he had not moved an inch. Wolves are still rampant in this region and the animals need to be guarded by day and locked up at night. I was satiated not only by the food but by the experience, and asked Sasha to pause at the top of the mountain pass for the final look at the range behind us: immense, smouldering, tumbling, smoky shapes of hills and mountains in the distance, with details lit by the shafts of fading sunlight, catching the roofs of a village in a valley far below. Echoes of barking dogs were wafted by the wind towards us. And then that heart-stopping moment as I raised my eyes and saw the peaks of the Caucasus *above* the clouds.

When we reached Kislovodsk, Yuri broke the silence with a vehement cry – '*Every day in life should be like this one!*' But I knew it had been exceptional.

EPILOGUE

In order to reach Istanbul, my next destination, I had to return to Tblisi and Moscow and catch my flight from there. A week later I was back in London having a cheerful reunion dinner with Gilbert & George and James Birch in the Groucho Club. They had just returned from America and were so full of it that I felt a pang of regret until Gilbert, with that sudden glint, leant towards me and exclaimed: 'New York was *fantastic*, but Moscow – Moscow will always be the *best!*'

The following afternoon I took the train towards my home in Devon and felt an odd elation as we sped through the English country-side, which basked in the warmth of the late spring day, passing an emerald field near Castle Cary speckled with black and white cattle. Such freshness would have made me gasp in Russia, but I had grown used to taking such scenes for granted in England because they were familiar. Now they twisted my heart. I wondered why; perhaps the contrast to Russia, the sense of infinite peace, the hedges, the ever-changing light unique to England.

Nothing was familiar any more. I have travelled far, but Moscow and the Caucasus were somehow different and I am still seeing things differently, one of the rewards for my time in Russia, which started with Gilbert & George in Moscow.

Our meeting was extraordinarily lucky for me. As one grows older, life tends to shrink, though I try to stretch it with new experience. Gilbert & George gave me this opportunity. Almost a year later, they continue to astound me.

North Devon, March 1991

With Gilbert & George in Moscow, 1990.

What is your favourite journey?
                FROM HEATHROW TO HOME

What is your present state of mind?
                VERY DISTURBED

                                        Gilbert & George
                                        19 April 1990
                                        Fournier Street

Bold type indicates illustration